FOREWORD

By: His Excellency
      Sam Terrence Condor
      (Former long-serving Deputy Prime Minister)
      Ambassador Extra-Ordinary and Plenipotentiary
      St. Kitts and Nevis

I am pleased to commend Michael S. Blake, a popular local educator of acclaim and accomplishment, on the release of his second literary work, 'Musings and Reflections 2 (Prose)'. This follows soon – mere months - of the success of his first publication.

I find the articles contained in this piece to be rather interesting, stimulating, thought-provoking, soul-searching, and, in one or two cases, even controversial.

It is, however, for me, a very positive development to note that this citizen of our Federation has joined the not-long-enough list of our very own grassroots writers and authors with the presentation of this book. I am certain that more of the same will follow.

I readily recommend possession and perusal of this book, and urge action on its call for active response.

May it serve the noble purpose for which it was penned.

From the Author

I am pleased to present 'Musings and Reflections 2' (Prose), a promised 'sibling' of its earlier opener, 'Musings and Reflections 1' (Poetry).

This opus is essentially a compilation of a series of speeches and articles, most of the latter hitherto unpublished, which have been delivered/ composed over the years, both as the consequence of an invitation so to do and as a response to developments, trends and 'AHA!' moments.

It is my firm, honest belief that the content of this publication can usefully serve as reference points for discussions, debates, research, theses, etc.

The topics treat several disciplines that affect and impact us in our personal, corporate, social, professional, spiritual and emotional lives, directly or otherwise.

It must be noted that since some of these essays were constructed, in several cases, more than a few years ago, some statistics might not hold true in a 2017 reality. Certainly, they were fully accurate and reflective of the time when the particular thesis was penned. Any seeming errors of fact, therefore, must be seen against that reality.

The above notwithstanding, I am confident that 'Musings and Reflections 2' (Prose) is worth the read!

A Call To And For Parents

A school of sociological thought sees parenthood as a social construct, defined to refer to the tasks, duties and responsibilities residing in and incumbent upon persons, usually adults, with minors in their charge and care. Correctly, in my view, parenthood differs from motherhood and fatherhood, which are quintessentially a product and conduct of biology.

For whereas all mothers and fathers ought and are expected to be parents, and in as much as the exercise of parenthood usually involves the discharge of functions normally associated with mother/fatherhood, the fact of the matter is that many, far too many biological mother and fathers do <u>not</u> parent their offspring, while many persons who never physically bore a child have served as excellent parents to myriad children.

But then, since the reality is that most, the vast majority, of children live with their mothers and/fathers, it follows that the functions of parenthood, without which a child cannot be taught or reared in the way that is right, must be exercised by these said mothers and fathers. It is an expectation that is fair, just and logical.

It also stands to reason, that because the behaviours, conduct, attitudes and values and tastes of very large portions and segments of our youth/student/child population are distasteful, unpalatable and obnoxious at best, that these socially unacceptable and morally abhorrent actions either mirror those exhibited by the mothers and fathers who 'rear' these children, or reflect a fundamental flaw in the parental model that these mothers and fathers display, or worse yet, are a combination of both deficiencies and dysfunctions.

Essentially then, it is clear that what our children need and deserve is not more or mere mothers and fathers, but rather more parenting, whether it comes from biological mothers or fathers, or others. (Many children live with and are reared by aunts, older siblings, uncles, god – parents, in laws, step relatives, and/or foster parents).

Good, proper parenting is a complex, time – consuming, energy - demanding, patience-exacting discipline that calls for consistency, persistency and insistency. It can only proceed or succeed where there is understanding of the tasks, and commitment and devotion thereto. It requires the possession and display of love, firmness, impartiality, compassion, justice, fairness, mercy, moral purpose, selflessness and accessibility, among other important traits and characteristics.

Real parents see to it that their children (biological or not, remember!) are exposed to education that is healthy, wholesome, relevant, and useful, and that such education, or its imparting is not at all left to the school (many of whose teachers themselves are poor parents!). As such, they ensure that decent, edifying reading material is readily available.

True parents ensure that the child's spiritual dimension is properly catered to by taking, or at least sending, him/her to church related services and activities. They pray for and with the child as a matter of course. They point the child to a love and service for the Creator by emphasizing His providence, and care and compassion as revealed in nature, beauty, family, food, music, art, and literature, among others. Proper parenting involves enlisting the child in volunteer, community service organizations, sporting activities and other talent – exacting, talent - honing enterprises.

The necessity and value of virtues such as teamwork, cooperation, respect, humility, industry, tolerance, sharing, honesty, decency, modesty, cleanliness, obedience to those in authority, dedication to task, discipline and stick-to-it-iveness are taught (both by precept and example) and demanded by good parents.

None can contest the proposition that (it is) what is said and done in the home, where parents hold sway, that tends toward the formation of habits and character more so that in any other setting, and that by and large, men are what their parents make them. The Bible, in Proverbs 22:6 (Train up a child, etc.) fully endorses this.

Who can dispute the contention that were children in general, including our students, subject and exposed to good parenting, or at least even better parenting than what currently obtains, our schools, our work places and society at large, would be infinitely sweeter, safer, more secure, more productive, and more effective?

The truth, unfortunately, is that many mothers in particular and fathers, too, have not at all graduated to being parents. And in their ignorance and naiveté, contentedly drop their calling and role to be parents on the schools in particular. But clearly, teachers cannot operate 'in loco parentis' if they themselves are not parents, as herein described. Parents must know that a child taught only at school is an uneducated child.

The time is right and ripe, no doubt, for institutions of teaching and learning to introduce 'PARENTING' as a discrete subject area, if only because these are centres that prepare students for adulthood, the work place, and for life, and it is certain that upwards of 90% of any given student cohort at any given time will produce at least a child sooner or later, when they are of adult and/or working age.

This educational innovation will, hopefully, and very probably, equip the rising generation with the knowledge, information and skills requisite for proper parenting, and in the process, save untold members of our boys and girls, our children, including generations yet born, from an otherwise yet unhealthy, unsavory existence that is nasty, brutish and short.

An Argument Against Gay Marriage

It is my considered opinion that in the Liberal vs Conservative debate on issues, each side at times presents a more reasoned, balanced, morally – acceptable and culturally-sanctioned view than the other. But with respect to same sex / gay marriage, the latter named position certainly holds fast and strong.

To be sure, there have been numerous cases of far-from-healthy, wholesome or savoury practices being bestowed with the cloak of legal legitimacy and social acceptance (smoking, common – law marriage, alcohol use, etc.) but in my books at least, for countries, cities and high profile 'leaders', presidents among them, to ascribe validity and acceptability to 'marriage' between a man and a man, and/ or between woman and woman, is to wallow in the filthy muck of the very lowest point of moral decadence and degeneracy.

There are innumerable, irrefragable scads of evidence residing in nature, religion, tradition, morality, common sense, social justice, physio-biological reality, basic decency and normalcy that consistently, unambiguously and insuperably contend against any argument that may be mounted pro gay marriage.

It is a perversion of, an aversion to and a diversion from right and rectitude of the highest order. The very idea of gay marriage, in my nostrils, stinks to high heaven like stale mackerel on a moonlight night.

Nature and religion, in particular, combine to present incontestable opposition to gay marriage. For even the smallest school boy, and the blindest of men, can see with pellucid clarity that the basic but very construct and design of the human anatomy simply do not allow for man to copulate with man, or woman with woman.

And I know of no religion whose official creed encourages or permits, far less commands man or woman to marry his/her own kind / sex. It is simply not meant to be.

Gay marriage has been rightly condemned as a threat to humanity's future, as a malignant microbe that has the potential to utterly destroy the fabric of the family, and as the epitome of anathema to right-thinking, normal people.

In my mind, the moves in many parts of the (notably Western!) world to legalize gay marriage is and will prove to be one of the most definitively retrograde steps taken in the history of civilization.

No society can preserve or sustain itself via same – sex marriage. Were it to become the norm, the new paradigm, humankind faces a limited future that culminates with inevitable atrophy and self destruction.

Of course, to allow for gay marriage demands a comprehensive redefining of the venerable institution of 'marriage', and a new definition of 'family', the oldest, most important and sacrosanct of human relationships and togetherness. The etymological, sociological, religious, cultural, social, and legal meaning of these two inextricably-intertwined human institutions will have to change to accommodate this decidedly satanic malpractice called same - sex marriage.

After all, it remains, and forever will remain impossible for a man to bear and deliver a child, as surely as it is for a woman to do so by engaging in 'coitus' with another woman. In addition, those 'liberals' who submit that a man/woman's decision to marry another man/woman is simply an exercise of choice must remember that freedom to choose implies and expects a freedom to choose right. And choosing wrong has always exacted a painful penalty.

Moreover, none can rebut the opposition that already, man really has no choice to marry as he chooses. He cannot choose to marry a child, an animal, his mother, his daughter, car or money, for example.

My position is that so-called gay persons are in serious need of guidance, counseling, help and reasoning. I do not subscribe to the theory that gayness is an unalterable, irreversible state of being. Gayness does not have to live forever.

As long as there is life, there's hope.

It seems to me that the way forward, the way to go is to work toward weaning and changing those who might be inclined to opt for gayness and/or gay marriage on to the straight and narrow path of man - with - woman, and woman- with – man relationships, --the difficulties, challenges and imperfections of these relationships notwithstanding.

Down with gay marriage!

British Royalty

The history of British Royalty spans almost 1200 years of human civilization, dating back to its first monarch in the person of King Alfred the Great, the first King of England, who reigned and ruled, from AD 671 to 899.

The current monarch, Queen Elizabeth II, who ascended the throne in 1952, is King Alfred's 32nd great granddaughter.

Over the years, the British Royal family has seen the Houses of Stuart, Orange, Tudor, Hanover and Windsor exercise reign over the Kingdom for different epochs in history. The current monarch is of the House of Windsor.

The present Kingdom of Great Britain, consisting of England, Scotland, Wales and Northern Ireland, was formed in 1707 by the Act of Union between England and Scotland.

Being a constitutional Monarchy and Parliamentary Democracy, the monarch of the kingdom currently reigns, but does not rule. Real power, and the responsibility of running the internal and external affairs of Great Britain resides in the cabinet, led by the Prime Minister, who practises what is commonly known as the Westminster Model or style of Government.

Over the years, Britain, a lower-medium-sized or upper small-sized nation, has exercised world clout far disproportionate to its size, punching way above its weight, so to speak. In the fields of politics, diplomacy, economics, culture, technology, the military, security, finance, education, science, medicine, sports, entertainment, aviation, and myriad others, Britain, despite or irrespective of who wears the Royal Crown, has for centuries been a major force on the world scene. In fact, Britain at one point ruled over an empire of a size unmatched by any other at any time. Its vastness was such that the sun never set thereon. It covered an area many multiple times that of the 'Mother Country'.

On every continent, in all directions, Britain was the controlling country, the owner, the ruler of many a colony, a host of which were several times her physical size. Indeed, of the ten (10) largest countries in the world in size, 5 of them (Canada, the USA (at the time the Thirteen North American Colonies), India, Australia and Sudan) were colonies of and ruled by Britain. This ensured that English became the only truly global language. Of course, Britain assumed ownership and control of more islands / territories in the Caribbean than any other power, and to this day, its influence is seen in our language, parliamentary system, economic patterns of development, large numbers of Caribbean people residing in the UK, cultural practices, educational systems, and styles of architecture, among others.

Importantly, the powerful symbolism of the British Monarchial system is retained in the Government Generalship of the many Caribbean nations, and in the Privy Council being the court of the last resort of even more of these said nations.

"Although 'guilty' is just one word, it usually means a long sentence."

Building Self – Esteem: Moving Children to Excellence

I am happy for this occasion to share with you some of my own thoughts on this matter of self-esteem and excellence, notwithstanding the fact that I stand here in loco parentis, in the trend of my superior.

You see, the question of excellence has almost always occupied my attention, to the point where I have had to seriously question whether this quality, this value we call excellence, has in fact been defenestrated along with so many of our traditional, tried and tested standards of decency, industry, morality, compassion and commitment in our personal, familial, professional and social lives.

We at the Ministry have become increasingly concerned at the rapid decline in the general level of excellence to which we had hitherto become accustomed.

Permit me to posit that we seem as a people here in St. Kitts in the Federation and beyond, to have replaced excellence with mediocrity, is far more real than imagined. Again and again, leaders in religion, business, government, diplomacy and education, in various forms, have lamented the fact that for too long now, too many of us have accepted the average as the norm, as our defining, acceptable standard. We have seen too many instances, far too many occasions wherein students are extolled and lauded for their 'excellence', when, in fact, by any objective or scientifically-recognized yardstick, the output is below par.

Of course, we are well aware as educators and parents of the need to validate and animate our students' and children's efforts and interventions. We must encourage our young people, and ever seek with judicious prudence and acumen to instil an, "I can do it" attitude in those whom we teach, rear and lead.

Yes, I cannot overstate that a sense of confidence builds self-esteem and facilitates a desire to try.

But we must not confuse the ordinary, the mundane, with excellence. We must be careful not to label mediocrity and "so-so" performance as being satisfactory or acceptable. The great, indomitable Plato was the one who declared many years ago that excellent things are rare. For a thing to be excellent, by this definition, by practice, if you please, it cannot be the norm, cannot be regular, cannot be ubiquitous or universal.

But the fact is that our students are in fact quite capable of excellence, pure and total. Perhaps not all of them, but I put it to you this morning that very many produce academic performances, display attitudes and output results that are definitely excellent, by any bench- mark. We have seen excellence in our times. What of Kim Collins, our other star sportsmen and women, our state scholars, our Scimatech productions, our farmers, our teachers, etc?

But to say it is not enough. We as teachers are called upon to create the environment and provide the wherewithal and animus for our students ever to excel. We must supply the material and implements with which students in turn, construct their world, the world of the future. And of course, we would not wish and want for that world to be safe, sane, prosperous and progressive.

The Ministry of Education hopes that this workshop will serve to equip you the participants with the tools, approaches and strategies requisite to facilitate and engender excellence.

We congratulate the co-ordinator and her team for covering this exercise and wish you all a successful, productive day.

Community Awareness of Adult Continuing Education (A.C.E) Opportunities and Service

I am of the opinion that the C.F.B College's decision to convene this symposium, at a time when the process of education enters another year and assumes new proportions, no doubt, is significant. For as the new academic year takes its place at the starting line, so to speak, it is inarguable, axiomatic even, that the question of education, the importance of education, the process of education, the matter of education, if you please, exact a new focus. Certainly, as we begin a New Year actively involved in the education enterprise, all of us stakeholders and shareholders therein recommit ourselves to the tasks at hand, wish for and anticipate great results.

Well, we must never lose sight of the fact that ACE is an integral, indispensable aspect of the education thrust. As Broadhead and Bloom (1996) would say, "any attempt to educate a people is inherently unstable and utterly incomplete if due and equal attention is not paid to the educational needs of the society's senior members; that is, those above and beyond compulsory school age." In fact, the very phrase "Continuing education" is no misnomer. It is not just academic jargon. For education, as well all know, is a life-long process, an unending activity. It continues ad infinitum.

So that having ACE in a deliberate, structured and organized manner is only fair. It stands to reason. It makes sense. Of course, this is not suggested that the modus operandi of all A.C.E must be formal. In fact, most of us here know that much, perhaps even most education and learning takes place in a non-formal or informal setting. We know, moreover, that many persons learn best, and some learn only in an environment that is not formal.

I say to you, then, those adults and their needs, however defined, must of necessity inform any plan or strategy devised, which is designed to improve the level of literacy and education in a society.

Here in St. Kitts, in recent times, and more and more, services in and opportunities for ACE abound. Again and again, time, expertise and resources are conscientiously set aside for this exercise.

That adults today, both young adults and senior adults, have infinitely greater access to educational opportunities, needs no defense or explanation. Nowadays, one can continue his education via attendance at colleges, universities, institutes, training centers, evening classes, and private home-tutoring, among others, all while staying planted in his home country.

But I am particularly concerned with ACE as it relates to those who would not have excelled at school, as it were, who would normally not qualify for matriculation into upper level institutions of higher learning.

For example, for many years now, the Education Department of the Ministry has been organizing and conducting evening classes and lessons in various disciplines; some academic, some not; specifically designed for adults of our communities.

Ladies and gentlemen, Evening Institute classes have been a conspicuous vista on our educational landscape for years. Additionally, several individuals, myself included, have for some time devoted significant portions of our after-regular-work-hours to ACE. Sometimes, some of us offer such services for free, sometimes at token cost, sometimes for more.

In a manner of speaking now, churches and church groups, institutes, academics and business houses have "joined the crew", and these units, together with private individuals and government entities such as CFBC, offer a wide array of opportunities and services in ACE. The content of this education run the gamut of the education process for illiterates, helping others with the barest qualifications to improve thereon, and providing the platform for those more advanced to further propel themselves educationally.

In this connection, the truth of the matter that one is never too old to learn, never too advanced in age to benefit from formal education, must be emphasized.

If I may, allow me to cite a case in point to document that claim: One of my very own ACE students, Mrs. Iva Stevens of Saddlers Village, sat the G.C.E.O level exam in English, last year. Imagine my utter delight and joy unspeakable when this 59-year-old grandmother obtained the highest score possible in the exam – grade A. Yes; this senior citizen took full advantage of an opportunity in ACE.

Yet, in spite of rare success stories like this one, despite the fact that opportunities and services do exist, and notwithstanding the satisfaction derived from knowing that many adults have benefited, some immensely, from ACE activities, I sometimes still wonder if enough of our communities are aware of such.

Does the number of registrants for ACE reflect a satisfactory level of awareness of the opportunities and services available? And are these numbers evenly distributed across our communities, or are urban dwellers and females disproportionately represented? With respect to our senior adults, is any (educational) needs assessment undertaken?

How about feedback, evaluation and follow up? I suggest, in fact, I submit, that these are areas crying out for attention, and perhaps the ACE division of CFBC could rise to the occasion.

Be that as it is, Ladies and gentlemen, as a facilitator of adult learning myself, I submit to you this evening that we must really be careful not to fall into the trap of being so obsessed with Primary and Secondary Education and all they entail, important as they may be, as to sideline the need to address ACE at the community level, particularly aimed, on occasions, at senior adults.

We must, individually and collectively, devote quality time and effort to ACE. When we do that, when we judiciously create more and more opportunities and services in ACE, and ensure that the entire community is aware of them and can readily access them, we in fact contribute to a paradigm shift in education, and we lend strength to Cooper and Cooper (1996). In their words, "…an educated adult presents a better role model in society. He is a better parent, a better worker, a better neighbor, a better citizen. He aids in shaping better youth and better children, who, in turn, make a better community and a better world."

My thoughts exactly.

Shalom!

"What you learn yourself matters much more than what others teach you."

"Never let a fool kiss you, and never let a kiss fool you!"

Developmental Programming for Culture and Identity in St. Kitts

It is the rule rather than the exception that in my travels abroad, and as a consequence of the resulting linkages and communications established, I am questioned as to my ethnic origin, my racial constitution, my nationality, my culture. Again and again, I am forced to question my answers in the aftermath of such interrogation. At times, I ponder the authenticity and worth, if any, of my culture and identity, and the nexus between the two.

I am confident that my assertion that today Kittitians are confused at best about this issue needs no defense. And this situation obtains in 1996, more than 500 years since the original natives of this land discovered Europeans on their soil; more than 160 years ago since our ethnic forebears were emancipated from the dirty institution of slavery; almost 60 years since local individuals began, as politicians, influencing socio-cultural behavior; and 20 years plus after political sovereignty, so-called.

Some might question the relevance of raising this matter of culture and identity in the presence of rising crime and violence, cost of living, unemployment, frivolous political issues and other seemingly more pressing ills.

Of course, the nature of culture is such that it shapes the development of the society and its constituents in all directions, and thus helps fashion whatever identity there is.

What are the characteristics of Kittitian culture? To what factors is our identity fixed? It seems to me that an answer to these questions implies at least that our own self - image is invalid.

This is because it is difficult at times to pin-point any particular mannerism of ours that can be described as originally, strictly and uniquely Kittitian. I am not very ready and willing to posit that 'cultural imperialism', the unbridled, unmitigated onslaught of foreign tastes and values being imposed upon us via the print and electronic media, is the sole culprit in the erosion of self-esteem, cultural identity and a sense of unique belonging. Other incidences, other structures converge to lend credence to the contention that we have no culture , that culture is for the elite, and/or that culture – or anything that is first class, in fact – comes from the 'First World'. These notions are a part of the wider debate that proposes that the 'Third World' has no legitimate claim to a culture, that everything that it has is a derivative of some sort and to some extent of what was originally external.

Space does not allow for a full, thorough discussion of the origin and ramifications of these fallacies, or for a rebuttal of the same, but we must admit, and it must be emphasized, that when a society is intellectually sterile, emotionally traumatized, politically immature, economically destitute and spiritually anemic, the manifest symptoms of which are becoming increasingly visible here, such misconceptions are nourished.

There is, admittedly, some truth in the claim that stripped of all its foreign content and reduced to its bare essentials, Caribbean culture in general leaves little that's exclusively ours. For example, many of us of African ancestry have grown to actually hate our heritage, and find comfort in identifying with the other 'society'. Many Kittitians still harbour ambiguities and erroneous perceptions of their role in the development of their locale and of mankind.

How often have teachers, scholars, academics and historians , among others, complained that the present recount of past events depicts and exaggerates the exploits and achievements of European and American 'heroes', to the bitter exclusion of local and regional stalwarts?

In fact, in my mind, it is this re-writing of history, so to speak, a re-ordering of priorities and emphasis vis-a-vis education and political and economic behaviour that is fundamental to the cure for our crisis of culture and identity.

We must begin to see images of dignity in our ethnic and racial origins, in our collective consciousness, and in our peculiar ways of doing things.

To achieve these lofty aims and realize these noble objectives, programme planning, implementation and development are not just mere addenda in this respect. They are absolute pre-requisites.

Cultural development must, as a matter of course, include and involve an acute awareness on the part of the populace-at-large of the various dimensions of culture, and their sum significance in a society's scheme of things. Developing activities and planning of things cultural must run the gamut of the educational, political, economic and religious spheres of a people's life.

Thus, the process of cultural planning and development must emphasize the development of the individual, shaping his thought patterns, influencing his tastes, values, outlook, attitude, behaviour and expectations.

For a person – a society – to be truly cultural, there must be constant reminders, including aural, visual, gustatory, tactile and olfactory, of what constitutes his cultural make up. Programming activities must, consequently, bear in mind the necessity of instilling in their participants and target audience, the importance of practising these specific cultural behaviours and ensuring their reinforcement and continuity by handing them down to their progeny, in as unadulterated a manner as possible.

This latter aspect of cultural enrichment must be deliberate and systematic. Children must know why they are being taught these particular habits, and why they are expected to cherish them and in turn pass them on to their offspring.

Culture, of course, works in tandem with history, politics, religion and economics to identify and define a people, and thus to posit that the programming, planning and development of culture in St. Kitts, as elsewhere, are of paramount importance, needs no defence, no further explanation.

It is sincerely hoped that this course will facilitate and precipitate this process of cultural growth in St. Kitts.

"Unless one knows what he wants, he stands very little chance of getting it."

"Some persons complain that they never get what is due to them; they should be glad they do not!"

"To make the best of old age, one has to start young."

Eliminate the Lunatics!!
(The case for discipline at our high schools)

It is manifestly the case today that all is not well at any of our high schools in St. Kitts. In a general sense, there is much room for amelioration (and I suppose this is applicable to numberless situations), but specifically with respect to discipline among the student populace, the institution is akin to a moribund asylum.

Certainly, the factors that predispose to this sad state of affairs find their roots not in any singular particular circumstance, but rather in the convergence and confluence of a multiplicity of trends and realities.

But notwithstanding the multifariousness of this cause of the lack of discipline, I am satisfied that it is nether inaccurate nor indefensible to posit that some factors, conspicuous or unequivocal, are to shoulder more of the blame for the current situation than others.

Discipline, in my mind, is no more mental idea, verbal concoction or metaphysical abstraction. It is a quality that lives itself out and concretizes itself in decent, responsible, uplifting behaviour. Sure, the term might be polysemic. Inarguably, it is an issue that is both relative and subjective. But in which school on earth is back-talking the teacher, 'sucking the teeth' at him / her, and flouting the teacher's orders with arrogance and abandon, considered anything less than indiscipline, pure and simple?

These, inter alia, abound at our high schools. And their profuse and unmitigated practice serves only to inhibit the school's basic function and stymie the realization of its objectives. You see, our societies have evolved to the crucial phase in history when young people – epitomized by students more than by any other group - , are re-acting, justifiably, or otherwise- , sometimes violently, against traditional values and any/all forms of authority. These rising multitudes who constitute the student body here at our schools are part and parcel of this trend. The school is theoretically a melting pot of social attitudes and values, but for too many of these students, their attitudes are too hard, too firmly embedded in the rock of intolerance, egotism, and obstinacy to be even thawed by the school's eclectic nature and the 'heat' that rises therefrom.

This is the problem that confronts the teachers and administrators at the school. The 'rebellion' of these young people against what they deem and dub encroachments on their 'rights' (this is not a deliberate, reasoned conclusion on their part, but is rather a spontaneous, natural reaction), essentially translates into ill-discipline, almost all the time.

But is enough being done to counter it? Is it being effectively or even properly dealt with? Are the students punished, disciplined for their errant ways? And if they are, does the punishment fit the crime?

The utilitarian school of thought reminds us that the certainty of punishment, even more than its severity, is the preventative of crime and wrong doing. I submit that the absence of such a certainty vitiates the teaching/learning process and frustrates the well-intentioned teacher, whose carefully-devised and artfully-executed lesson is rudely interrupted by some empty headed, dimwitted, foul-mouthed, untrained brat.

Punishment, in essence, is justice for the unjust, pens the illustrious St. Augustine of Hippo. Perhaps the administrators of our high schools ought to ponder that. I firmly believe that there is redeeming value in corporal punishment.

I make no bones about my support for Otto Von Bismarck who thunders that wrongdoers should 'stew in their own grease'.

It is abundantly clear that the recidivism in misbehavior and ill-discipline at our school obviates the verbal reprimand and suspensions which pass for 'punishment' at the institutions.

Teachers, here as elsewhere, have the peculiar and unenviable task of inculcating knowledge while at the same time breaking down insubordinate resistance to its inculcation. The ensuing struggle borders on lunacy.

The system that operates here at our schools vis-à-vis punishment and discipline of our students runs counter to and makes a mockery of the fundamental tenets of pedagogy, scholarship or logic. A pattern of misconduct, sometimes subtle, often undisguised, and in myriad forms, runs the gamut of the school population and represents a seething sub-cultural underbelly of the body politic.

And the majority of teachers resent it. To be sure, their general silence about it is deafening. Their reluctance to ventilate their views on the matter is cowardly and unprofessional. But that there is much indiscipline, compounded, and herein, I repeat, is the crux of the problem – compounded by an unmistakably inept dealing with it -, needs not be laboured.

Teachers did not invent the system. Nor do we run it. Its modus operandi, its anima vivendi, its structure and effects are too woefully inefficient, archaic and regressive to have been the work of a body as intelligent as teachers. But here at our schools, the teachers demand and deserve that the students whose conduct is rotten to the core, be appropriately and expeditiously arrested and punished. The shoddy treatment of offenders constitutes tolerance of, perhaps indirect animus to their misdeeds. And he who tolerates evil is worse than he who perpetrates it.

Albert Einstein concludes for me: "It is essential that the students acquire an understanding and lively feeling for discipline. Otherwise, he ………. more closely resembles a sub-human being whose behaviour does not even approximate that of a well – trained dog"!

Humble suggestions are punishment for misconduct at our schools are in order here:

Almighty God Himself recommends, in fact orders, punishment.

Punishment must be consistent, impartial, and expeditiously meted out.

Punishment must not only be done; it must be seen to be done.

Punishment is actually the dispensing of justice. And justice without force is impotent.

Favouritism, nepotism and familiarism must not stand in the way of punishment. The guilty student must not be, or made to feel that he/she is being, pampered, petted or coddled.

Means of punishment could/should include:

Physical beating
Suspension
Expulsion
Cleaning – thoroughly! – the classrooms and/or school compound
Denial of certain privileges such as participating in P.E, Field trips, Club Meetings and activities, School sports, etc.
Removal from positions of leadership (class captains, prefects, club leaders)
Kneeling
Lines
Properly organized and supervised meaningful detention
Written and/or verbal apology to offended party in the presence of the class or entire school
Withdrawal of lunch and/or break intervals
Record to be made on culprits' file re nature of indiscipline

ENVIRONMENTAL BLIGHTS – WHAT ARE WE DOING ABOUT THEM?

There is hardly any street anywhere in Basseterre (and the same holds for many other communities on the island) which does not count among the structures that define it a number of unoccupied, abandoned, dis-used, dilapidated or dirty buildings, largely edifices constructed and meant as dwelling houses.

This is a sorry state of affairs that has been an unpalatable part of our housing landscape for decades, and its content and extent, clearly, are expanding.

It seems ironic, almost comical, that even as government, business and private agencies engage in a frenetic and endless pace of home construction, which end products are gobbled up by home-hungry residents and others long before they are completed, an in an environment where, under normal circumstances, a house does not remain on rent for more than a day before it is occupied by new tenants, the number of houses/former houses and other buildings becoming or remaining idle increases significantly.

But the practice of allowing these architectural-specimens-gone-awry to litter our landscape, has, in my own estimation, reached obscene, untenable, intolerable proportions, and demands our immediate collective attention and action, for a number of compelling reasons.

Certainly, the aesthetic beauty of the street/area is severely contaminated, as many of these erstwhile homes et al are veritable eyesores, enveloped as many of them are in bee-bush and other weeds. Simultaneously, the otherwise eye-pleasing style, appearance and décor of inhabited neighbouring houses are compromised, at times seemingly neutralized, by these adjacent derelicts.

Of course, the market value of the potentially costly in-use houses is significantly diminished, juxtaposed, as they are, against the eye sores.

In addition, and as is well known, these abandoned buildings become repositories for/ of garbage and refuse, overtime emitting a foul, putrid stench that is decidedly deleterious to one's health, and serves, naturally, to attract rodents, vermin, insects and pests (particularly cockroaches, rats and mosquitoes) that compound the problem by spreading disease and discomfort.

Moreover, in far more than a few instances, not only are squatters and vagrants 'invited' to set up camp, so to speak, bringing with them their generally unhealthy, unwholesome, unwanted practices and behaviours, but, undoubtedly worse is the fact that criminals, too, take up physical residence, loaded, of course, with their drugs and weapons. At the very least, they hide and/or store them there.

How often do we read or hear of the police finding narcotics, guns, ammunition in an 'abandoned' building? Further, in some areas, these said pieces of property are converted into whorehouses, where transactional and prostitution sex occurs on a regular basis. So that it is transparently clear that these many and growing-in-number unattended-to buildings serve a number of grave negatives, including reducing the quality of life of/ for residents and occupants of nearby houses, promoting the proliferation of pests and their accompanying diseases, depreciating the worth of occupied of otherwise – valuable neighbouring properties, facilitating the housing of crime, criminals and vagrants, and indeed, depriving many persons genuinely in the need of land or houses from accessing such, as they occupy otherwise useful tracts of real estate.

Our concern, born of the unambiguously clear implications of this growing trend, is that the relevant authorities/ powers of the land are entirely inattentive, inactive and unresponsive to what is clearly an undesirable but increasing phenomenom.

It is vehemently recommended and urged that, where it does not exist, the appropriate legislation be enacted and acted upon to either oblige and compel owners to address the issue (by clearing the land and/or buildings in a decent, environmentally friendly condition; by tearing down these houses, etc. that are beyond repair; by selling the properties; by donating said properties to the State or some charity or other person/ group; or by forfeiting ownership of the property as a result of failure to apply any of the foregoing within reasonable time!) Where the necessary legal authority or framework already exists, it must be strengthened and enforced forthwith, without fear or favour.

Of course, government always reserves the right to expropriate property for the public good under certain conditions. And it is true that in a number of cases, these abandoned buildings, etc, these conditions do exist.

Let us hope that serious, consistent, effective action is taken with regards to these many abandoned, derelict houses and other building s in St. Kitts, this year of our Lord 2011.

"One reason why so many do not recognize opportunity is that it is often disguised as hard work."

HOOLIGANISM IN SPORTS

The recent troubling incidents of violence on the fields of the 1st Division football matches are reminiscent of the hooliganism that characterizes soccer engagements in Europe, especially when British fans are among the spectators. Such incidences always result in injury to a number of spectators and bystanders, and sometimes find their end in death for some.

It must be stressed early that to continue the demonstration of the pugnacious capacity of our young men during the local games will eventually lead to an extension in magnitude and nature of the same, and such a development can only redound to the disadvantage of the hitherto popular sport.

One concerned person has already lamented the seeming demise of the netball entity in Nevis, and although the factors that predisposed to the sorry state of affairs there differ from those that now menace the survival of football here, the consequences will be the same: the cessation of a popular form of entertainment for many.

All sports, football included, should aim to develop teamwork and discipline among its participants, build (their) physical fitness, and, most certainly, provide a legitimate means of having wholesome, healthy fun. But there is another element in this exercise that is almost never stressed: the missing dimension to the sports panorama here in SK and abroad is the rotten lack of sportsmanship, the absence of ethics in the sports process.

The reliance and super-emphasis on winning causes many players to regard their rivals as expendable units, as antagonists and bitter competitors for first place.

And even, as is supposedly the case, this view by the players is temporary, lasting only as long as the game; even if we agree, as we must, that keen competition makes for an exciting, skill-exhibiting, enjoyable game, we must conclude that if the unbridled lust for victory - at - all - cost is allowed to run amok, the beauty of the game will suffer, as players deliberately seek to incapacitate and hurt opponents, and violence ebbs and flows.

Couple this 'unsportsmanlike' attitude and aggressive approach with shoddy, shabby or sloppy officiating by referees and linesmen, and we have the winning recipe for losing the game as a demonstration of a skill and talent.

The police, too, must discharge its role. Sure, as individuals, they, too, have their heroes, stars and favourites, but when they are in uniform during match time, their unequivocal and overriding duty should be to ensure that violence, especially involving spectators, of the type we've now been introduced to, is contained to its barest minimum. Plain-clothed police officers are also bound to intervene to limit the chances of any disagreement among spectators or players bulging into a show-down. The relevant governing body must swiftly, strictly and consistently apply whatever measures are legitimate and appropriate to players, and to referees and linesmen, who deliberately provoke or initiate acts of aggression and/or unfair play on the field. The glory of the sport survives better without such hicks and would-be gladiators.

Sports and the exercise they afford are beneficial and relaxing, and football is an integral aspect of our sports culture and calendar. But I'd prefer not to have any football at all than have it marred and animalized by continued lousy refereeing, players' lack of sportsmanship, and spectators' unruly behaviour. Let us root out this virus now.

"Power will, sooner or later, intoxicate the best hearts."

Madame Chairman and President of the Board of Directors, Registrar of Cooperatives

Thank you most sincerely for your kind invitation to the Ministry of Education to grace this august event with its presence and to participate actively in a real sense, by presenting brief remarks.

It is my singular honour and privilege to represent the M.O.E on this occasion, and to bring you greetings from the Honourable Minister, the C.E.O and the Ministry at large.

Ladies and gentlemen, you would commiserate with me, I expect, if this abbreviated presentation is not punctuated by the kind of slant and/or informational content you may have become accustomed to, but this is because this task was assigned to me at the eleventh hour, so to speak.

But I wish to say with unambiguous clarity that the Ministry recognizes the very significant role which the cooperative movement in general and the School's Apex Society, in particular, has played and continue to play in the multi – pronged approach of the Ministry to facilitate all-round development of our people, specifically that of the rising generation, inevitably and irrevocably the men and women of tomorrow, and hopefully,   - for it is neither automatic nor axiomatic   - , the leaders of that morrow.

You see, Madame Chairman, those of us in education and especially if we are dually blessed with the privilege of parenting, have come to recognize, and readily admit, that whereas our students today will as a matter of fact age and mature into the adults of the future, a natural evolution that is as certain as night follows day, the same does not at all apply to their becoming leaders.

For although the truth is that many of us so very often glibly declare that the children and youth of today, our students, if you please, are the leaders of tomorrow, the fact of the matter is that, in large measure, that is not necessarily so.

The point is, that leadership is neither inherited nor ascribed. Shakespeare opined in Twelvth Night, Act II, that some are born great; implying, I believe, that those so fortunate are natural leaders.

Tacitus, however, is of the belief that leadership is instilled, not given. Leadership must be honed, he submits. One must be trained, guided, taught, if he is to lead right and lead well.

And herein lies one of the major strengths of the co-operative movement. It instills qualities and principles of leadership in and among its participants, members and adherents in its modus operandi.

For example, we believe that a function of the co-op programme is manifested in the fact that it teaches thrift.

And this is critical. In an age of much spoilage, wastage, and corrupt patronage, the instilling of this value in our young people is commendable indeed.

By encouraging students to save, and providing the avenue to do so, the cooperative movement is directly imparting to them the wisdom of economizing and investing.

And, by extension, this fosters a spirit of entrepreneurship, promotes self-reliance, and builds an enabling environment for the flourishing of self-esteem.

All of this, we dare say, strengthens internal as much as fiscal discipline, and in turn constructs an edifice wherein leadership can thrive.

The Ministry is also proud to be part of this morning's ceremony because it takes careful note of the report of the School's Apex Cooperative Society Ltd., wherein it boasts of a net surplus in its operations, the dividends of which are distributed among its many shareholders, of course.

This tells me that the co-op is well run, and congratulations are in order for the president, executive body, management team and members. Almost all schools are involved in the society. We note the growth in the membership of the entity. It is clearly over the 3000 mark, a good and promising sign, if you ask me.

Naturally, I venture to declare, the Ministry is well pleased that several of its employees, teachers, in fact, are so directly and actively engaged in the business of the co-op operation, helping, as it were to shape our students' minds and sharpening their business savvy in the right direction.

I am commissioned to extend to all of you, the M.O.E's heartiest and heartfelt gratitude, thanks, appreciation, commendation and best wishes for a superlatively successful 26th annual general meeting, and may the blessings of God Almighty continue to attend and cover you individually and as a collective unit.

Thank you very much.

"It is better that a student have no teacher at all than his having a poor or bad teacher."

"True safety consists not in the absence of danger, but in the presence of God."

WOMEN HAVE LOST THEIR DIGNITY!

It is manifestly the case that femininity is, generally speaking, not just under threat. It is being routed to oblivion on a massive and sometimes rapid scale.

What is particularly strikingly – and worrying – about this unpalatable phenomenon, however, is the fact that those who are guilty of a colossal onslaught against feminine dignity, include, believe it or not, women themselves.

In recent times, the fashionable thing to do has been to berate and chastise young men in particular for their deviant, non – conformist, violent and sociopathic behaviours. And, I contend, rightly so.

Again and again, social scientists, politicians, preachers, teachers, law – enforcement agents, parents and the society at large have damned and derided the statistics – supported tendency of boys of school age and young adult males to be truant, aggressive, recalcitrant, obdurate, and idle, thereby marginalizing themselves.

We have had the time of our lives, as it were, devising mechanisms and deploying strategies to deal with what we collectively consider to be a rising tide of male – initiated crime and violence.

And we do all this with scant regard to or mention of our concern for the clear and marked slide into decay and degeneracy of our female folk.

But any objective observation, examination or analysis of contemporary female trends and behaviours must leave us with spasms of genuine concern.

For example, it is fairly common to see girls/young women standing, walking, and sitting with little thought or concern of personal privacy and dignity. Their speech, more often than not, is laced with expletives and degrading, offensive content that easily rivals that of their male counterparts.

As per their style and mode of dress, clearly, the slogan of the hour and the order of the day is 'how low can you go'.

Females in general, but certainly especially younger females, are just as guilty of 'mansprawling' (sitting with feet very wide apart) as men themselves, and this irrespective of their attire.

Certaintly, our judaeo-christain ethic must be impugned, insulted even, by skirts and pants the deliberately expose females' belly button, entire midriff section, and underwear.

Couple this with blouses that reveal abundant cleavage, underarm hair, and more, and we are presented with a package of indecency that borders on the obscene and vulgar.

But women (they certainly do not meet the criteria for 'lady'–hood) must understand that whereas perhaps initially this type of walking and dressing was provocative , they have become so commonplace and crude that they no longer tickle men's fancy.

Moreover, they must know that such styles of dress and speech actually turn off decent – minded men with good intentions; are in fact a bane to women's health and reputation; give the impression that they are cheapskates; and represent a sub-cultural underbelly of the body politic.

Most certainly, I would not sanction my daughter's subscribing to that type of behaviour or dress, and would actively discourage my many sisters from doing so.

So that while the country by and large preoccupies itself with focusing on the negative behaviours of our boys and young men, we ignore the creeping and expanding negative behaviours of our girls and young women, to our peril.

Indeed, the silence of the more cultured and 'refined' of our lady – folk with respect to this degradation of the female esteem and personhood, is thunderous and strange.

Advancing Child Protection: Controlling Truancy and Non–Attendance at Schools

Presented: Tuesday 25th July, 2006. 10:20 a.m
Sugar Bay Club, Frigate Bay
(Probation & Child Protection Services Conference)

The Ministry of Education, which I am privileged and honoured to represent this morning, is pleased to be a part of this very relevant and germane activity organized by its sister Ministry of Social Development, Community and Gender Affairs. We in the Ministry of Education believe with the Minister of Social Development that given the socio-cultural reality of the day, and in light of the urgency of the times, that it is fundamentally critical that a regime which proffers a more effective and efficient multi-prolonged response to issues of child protection, be instituted as a matter of national priority.

In addition, given the complexity and intricacy of the nature of the challenge presented by the vexing issue of child protection, the Ministry of Education is concerned, and insists that our approach to this matter be neither crude nor infantile. In this connection and towards this end, the Ministry offers its services, expertise and resources, limited though they may be, towards the goal of ensuring that child protection in the Federation be a vital, critical element in a systematic, deliberate policy of security the welfare of children. Child protection, ladies and gentlemen, must be for us a normal state of affairs, a fait accompli.

I wish therefore to take a few minutes to expatiate a bit on some ideas as to how controlling truancy from and non-attendance at school ought to be and in fact does constitute one of those prongs in the multi–faceted approach to child protection.

The Education Act No.9 of 2005, to which I shall refer from time to time during this discourse, is the legal document, which, in a real sense, guides and governs the Education system in the Federation.

It devotes two entire Divisions (3 & 4) to the issue of attendance at schools for children of school age.

With respect to the matter at hand, therefore, the Act is quite articulate and instructive. In Part 3, Division 3, Section 26, Subsection 1, for example , the Act makes clear that "Every child shall attend school from the beginning of the school calendar in the school year ………..until the last of the school calendar in the school year in which the child attains sixteen years of age………..".

By law, then, children in and of the Federation between 5 and 16 years of age are to be in school when school is on. It is as simple as that. Or is it? We shall see.

Truancy is loosely defined as the unauthorized absence from school or from class sessions by a student. By 'unauthorized', we mean that neither the school, a medical doctor, the Court, nor his legal parents / guardians gave him, the child, legitimate permission to be absent.

Again, the question of legitimacy is critical, as some parents' orders and instructions are in fact the raison d'être of truancy. More on this later.

In the 1970's and early 1980's, the prevailing socio-economic circumstances were such that many families found it difficult to prepare and present to their children of school age, adequate, nutritious, satisfying meals, particularly at mornings and at lunch time.

Perhaps, some may argue, this unpalatable state of being still exists. The fundamental difference between then and now, however, in respect of food availability is the fact of the appearance of the school meals programmme, introduced by the PAM Administration of the Right Honourable Dr. Kennedy Simmonds in the mid 1980's.

Education Officials noted that one of the immediate effects of the school-feeding exercise was a pronounced increase in attendance of students, especially at the primary level.

Of course, it was also interesting to observe that in some cases, students turned up at school not for or at 8.30 a.m, but just before lunchtime, although they tended by and large to remain thereafter for the afternoon session.

Clearly, one can deduce from the foregoing that there is still a need for some students to have access to a proper breakfast as well. And I am confident that, in time, that service will be provided to complement the lunch programme.

Records and statistics compiled by the Ministry since then show beyond a doubt, that the level of truancy has been reduced, significantly so, in some cases.

It was later recognized by the Ministry of Education that the access to and availability of a daily lunch notwithstanding, there would be some amount of internal truancy. That is, even though the child is on the physical premises, he is not inside the classroom, where he belongs, but rather roaming the corridors, climbing trees, occupying the toilets, etc.

Thus was born the SELF project – Student Education Learning Fund – , which provided and still provides free lunches, text books on loan to students for as long as they are needed, and pays the external examination fees for students.

All of us know that the current situation in our public schools is characterized by an abundance of freeness. An excess of freeness, if you ask me.

I have had reason to point out an reiterate that St. Kitts – Nevis is perhaps the only country on each where a students can attend school from being to end without it costing his parents a cent.

We provide free tuition, free furniture, free bus transport, free text books, free exam fees, free school meals, and, where necessary or requested, free uniforms.

It stands to the reason then, I submit, that any objective analysis of this plethora of freeness would lend and lead to the conclusion that there should in fact and in deed be absolutely minimal truancy in this mini – state of ours, in light of the fact, the very significant fact, that all the external stimuli, much extrinsic motivation, is in place.

And yet the fact of the matter is that there is still, in our estimation, plenteousness of truancy and abundance of non-attendance. Clearly, there is a missing element.

Let me here inform this august audience that the record indicates that, in a reversal of the pre-schools – meals norm, the problem of truancy and non attendances is increasingly becoming more acute among high/secondary school students than primary, and is infinitely more pronounced among males.

Let me pellucidly establish and settle the point that truancy does exist. Admittedly, and lamentably, there are no statistics that accurately measure either quantitatively or qualitatively the incidence of truancy at our schools.   This is except for the sometimes unreliable class registers, which purport to record who attends school on which day, and whether he/she is early. There is little else to go by.

Moreover, we have had cases, on far more than one occasion, where students are marked present, but for all intents and purposes, they are practically not in attendance at their respective lessons.

Heads of schools sometimes report that their school has no problem with truants, yet the reality is that the street corners, the Bayfront areas, the hills and valleys are littered with truant students, AWOL if you please, during school hours. And this in spite of the laws and regulations that indicate unambiguously that such a course of action ought not to be.

The truth is that, on occasions, heads of schools may not report someone as truant for fear that the relevant authorities may seek, locate, capture and return that student to school, and the school believes that it is actually better off without that particular student, given the fact that he may be a constant, persistent, repeat offender who causes intractable problems for the smooth, efficient running of the school.

And yet, despite the foregoing, the Ministry of Education finds it deplorable that, instead of seeking to remedy and rectify a problem – for clearly, truancy is a problem – it is being shirked.

We in the Ministry also contend that it is entirely unacceptable that after 40 long years of Universal Secondary Education, a feat unequalled in the OECS and unmatched by many in CARICOM , that persons of school age are found wanting re regular attendance at school.

The law of the land obliges and commands that that all citizens and residents of the Federation between 5 and 16 years of age <u>must</u> be in school. There is adequate space for all who are in that age category in our school system, which is aided and abetted, so to speak, by the fact that all facets of the delivery of education are free of cost, as earlier explained.

Ladies and gentlemen, why is the Ministry of Education so concerned about truancy and non-attendance? Why am I concerned? Why should you be concerned? Why?

Because truancy and non–attendance present a clear and present danger not only to the perpetrators who are, by the way, also victims themselves, but also to the education system, to social equilibrium, to the economic enterprise, and to the body politic.

Hughes and London (2002) found "a close relationship between chronic truancy, delinquency, and involvement in criminal and socio–pathic behaviours."

We are concerned because of the implications, ramifications and repercussions of this undesirable phenomenon. We are concerned because of the cost to society and to the economy occasioned by truancy and non–attendance. I say to you today that we are concerned because of the effects it has / they have on individuals, the family, school, government, the workplace and the economy.

When a child is truant while he is a student, later, as an uneducated, unskilled, untrained adult, he becomes not an asset, but a liability to the labour pool, extracting from the national basket that which he has not put in or contributed to, and robs the economy of the social capital it needs to develop, in the form of intellect, skills, expertise, competencies and attitudes.

Just as fundamentally, I need to emphasize, truancy runs counter to all four dimensions of Education's Mission, which include the academic/intellectual, technical/vocational, socio-cultural, and moral/ethical. . Truancy deprives and /or denies a child of his right to education, thereby stymieing his growth, particularly as it relates to his intellectual development.

Truancy and non -attendance are physically, financially, intellectually, socially and morally stultifying, regressive and deleterious. Most importantly, we are concerned that they lend and lead to abuse, to exploitation, including sexploitation, of all forms and types. Abuse, by its very nature and practice, is restrictive and inimical to one's academic, physical, emotional, economic, and spiritual health.

And so it is not only an academic exercise or rhetorical question to ask, "Why should truancy and non-attendance be controlled?"

I put it to you this morning without fear of contradiction that to control these twin monsters is to pre-empt and prevent abuse of the emotional, physical and psychological dimensions of the affected persons, both victim and perpetrator. To control these "terrible two" is, in a real sense, to secure the future. It saves children – our most precious, and from all appearances, our most abundant resource.

Eliminating truancy facilitates advancing child protection, and contributes to fulfilling the promise to have children enjoy the right to a decent education.

When we attempt to control truancy and non-attendance, we show an understanding of the problem and express sympathy (and for some of us, empathy). By essaying to control, we exemplify and concretize man's humanity to man, in the process proactively work towards preventing ignorance.

Remember, if we think education is expensive, we should try ignorance. This is why the Ministry of Education persists with making education freely available to and accessible by all our children. After all, as Confucius aptly reminds us, "Ignorance is the night of the mind, but a night without moon or stars." Darkness pure and total, in other words.

And so, yes, to labour point that we need collectively and assiduously to control truancy and non-attendance needs little defence or explanation.

Let us now briefly examine some of the salient factors that tend to predispose to and/or engender truancy and non-attendance. I put before you for consideration, the following possible contributors:

Absence of adequate laws, or lax laws 'on the books'
Non – enforcement of existing laws

A culture that encourages, or at the very least, does not actively condemn or report truancy.

Apathetic, indifferent, non-committed teachers

Ignorant, couldn't-be –bothered, ineffective police officers

Indisciplined, delinquent parents / guardians

An uninviting school environment, including a system structure that does not deal too kindly, in a manner of speaking, with non-academically-gifted / bent students

A weak familial, educational and /or spiritual foundation

Abuse, hunger, neglect

The clearly-prevailing attitude that at least some amount or type of truancy / non-attendance is acceptable.

These, ladies and gentlemen, I humbly suggest, represent some of the major variables influencing the presence of truancy and non-attendance at schools. No doubt there are others.

How do we control it (since, admittedly, it cannot be completely eradicated), however, is, in my mind, the crux of the matter.

Allow me to humbly but sincerely offer the following measures as elements and ingredients in the recipe for successful and effective control of the phenomena:

We must enact, or, where they already exist, strengthen laws that deliberately and specifically target these co-eval undesirables

We must call parents to account for the wanton and reckless truancy of their children / wards.

And let me here interject and emphasize the utterly important role of the male parent, the father, in this respect.

Yale University psychiatrist Dr. Kyle Purrett in 2005 found that "Children's social, physical and intellectual developments benefit greatly from the involvement of fathers………." He also reports, "Fatherless children are more prone to depression than are those with a father, are twice as likely to be school truants and dropouts, are more criminally active, and both inflict and experience abuse more than children with fathers………." Dr. Pruett continues, "Father deprivation is directly linked to difficulties in a child's life, including self-control, truancy, and violence."

And, if I may add, in my own experience as a teacher, Deputy Principal and Acting Principal, I have found that the vast majority of "troublemaking", trouble-giving and troublesome students flow from homes run by single parents, almost always a mother or grandmother. And so a clarion call is again being made to fathers to "get with it". Get directly, actively, permanently involved in the bringing of your children, particularly your sons. Help us control truancy!

In any event, the Act, in Section 36, obliges you as a parent, so to do. It states: "………it shall be the duty of the parent of every child of compulsory school age to cause the child to receive an education by regular attendance at school."

And, in fact, if you do not comply, Section 45 (1) addresses that, too: "A parent of a child of compulsory school age who neglects or refuses to cause the child to attend school,…………….. commits an offence ………….."

The third prong in controlling truancy and non-attendance is to thoroughly engage and train truancy officers.

As we understand it, all police offers are ex oficio truancy officers, but we are proposing a return to the situation wherein particular persons are selected, prepared and trained for a definite job description as truancy or school attendance officers, vested with all the requisite legal authority to bring truants to heel.

The Act, again, is instructive and helpful in this regard when it speaks to this issue in Sections 39, 40 (b), and 41. It in essence bestows on such officers the legal authority to investigate cases of truancy and report guilty students and parents, and makes it an offence for any person to assault or obstruct said officers in the execution of their duty.

There is a crying, urgent need to make education, as it pertains to its content, delivery and modus operandi , more attractive, more relevant, more participative, more student – centered, more child –friendly, less academically-oriented, less competitive.

We believe that this would encourage more and better attendance, and reduce truancy. We must install safety nets and support systems, including guidance and counseling services, for both students and parents. We need partnerships and liaisons with other stakeholders in grappling with this matter. We must have Education, in tandem with the Police, Probation Officers, School Attendance Officers and the general public, working together cooperatively, collaboratively and constructively.

We must judiciously create conditions that conduce to best practice for institutional strengthening, students' empowerment and positive outcomes.

I genuinely believe that truancy can be controlled. But this objective cannot be realized if all sectors of society, including all the stakeholders in education and youth, do not combine and converge and work assiduously towards its end.

Ladies and gentlemen, we are cognizant of the maxim, and verily believe, that what its children become, that will the community become. What's done to children, they will do to the society.

Children must be made to see the worthlessness, the uselessness, the danger of truancy and non- attendance at school in the immediate, medium and long term , and to appreciate the value and worth of being in school, learning as much as they can for as long as they can in all the ways that they can.

I believe that given our track record of innovations, interventions and introductions on behalf of our children, our students, our youth, coupled with a commitment to tackle the task, and enjoined by an abiding faith in God, we can, since we must control with a view to eliminating from our fair land, the unsightly, dangerous spectacle of truancy and non-attendance.

I call on all of you, on all of us, to get to work immediately and commitedly towards this end. Thank you for listening.

Subject: Social Studies
Topic: The Treatment of the aged in a society is culture- based, and has implications for all who grow old in that society.

Date: 18th May, 1983.

It is indeed an apodictic truism that whatever a society does is reflective of its values and indicative of its cultural traits and modes. This includes not only the way the people of that society live, their food, music, dress and the nature and structure of its institutions, but, indeed, it includes also actions of a more moral plane and subjective nature, such as the treatment it gives to the aged among and in it.

Whatever the nature and result of this treatment, however, it has serious, strong implications for the people who do grow old in that society. After all, it is they to whom this treatment will be meted out in the process of time.

From the very beginnings of time, in all societies, old people therein have been treated differently, for better or for worse, but differently, from the rest of the populace. More over, and intrinsically, the definition of age varies from society to society, and each society defines and treats the aged according to its particular culture.

In fact, therein lies the reason why aged people are not treated similarly everywhere: this treatment is culture – based, and no two cultures are facsimiles of each other.

It seems imperative to mention that in some societies agedness is not determined purely or exclusively by chronological age. In any event, that would be impractical, for what is the difference between the fifty-year-old man who looks at least fifteen years older than his age, and is as weak, poor, helpless, dependent, and/or incapacitated as the seventy –five-year old neighbour? Geriatricians, I am sure, will insist that both of them have the characteristics of aged people, and should thus be treated as such. Moreover, such cases (as that of a 50 -year old being as feeble as an 80-year old) are not mere hypothetical suppositions, for in the 'Third World', for instance, lack of familial care or companionship, disease, sickness or grinding poverty can render a man physically weak and mentally depressed, adding a few years on him/her in a matter of weeks and months. The effects of alcohol and cigarettes also tend to precipitate old /age in a large number of individuals.

So that if we take St. Kitts for example, we find that the age at which someone is considered old/ aged is not necessarily the same as that of Santa Domingo, Colombia, the United States, or India. This is rather self – explanatory, because, needless to emphasize, people age faster and more visibly in some societies and in some climates than in others. This can be due to environmental, economic or health factors, or a combination thereof.

But then, even if a person is considered aged say in St. Kitts at age 65, 85 in the United States, 50 in Chad and 80 in South East Asia, that person is given different specific treatment in each society. The culture of each dictates the difference in treatment.

This treatment can be planned, deliberate, systematic and/or calculated, or it can be spontaneous or sub – conscious. In societies where culture allows for the former type, one often finds that as soon as the process of aging begins to exhibit itself in a pronounced manner, the individuals in question are taken to special homes where the facilities are designed to help them live the latter period of their lives in relative ease and comfort. (Provided of course, that these people have no concerned relatives who are able and willing to accommodate them, the State, depending on the nature of the society and its culture, assumes the responsibility of caring for these aged ones). This duty becomes more incumbent upon its executors especially if the beneficiaries worked diligently and honestly during the years of productivity. Cuba, other communist countries, and Swaziland are the leading examples of countries whose culture – base is so structured.

There are also those countries for which, it would seem, it is a burden and a bother, apart from being a strain on their resources, to care for 'non-productive' citizens and residents. Aged people in these cultures, such as Uganda and Haiti, suffer immensely and die in the early stages of their agedness. There is no public outcry of concern, protest, etc, at this type of treatment. And why, after all? It's their culture.

Yet, other societies, such as that of St. Kitts, seems to let things run their course, intervening on the behalf of the aged only and not until the individual becomes a threat or a severe nuisance to the rest of the society by undesirable acts such as continual begging, theft, harassment of others, or becoming an unkempt, unhealthy sight (especially if tourists complain). Some might argue that given our economic reality, the state cannot do better than render last minute assistance, but I contend that first and foremost, our cultural values must be changed and redirected to the point where it is seen as a moral, compelling, civic duty to properly house, clothe, and feed the aged in society.

In St. Kitts, for example, knocking down an aged person (with a vehicle) is "no big thing" so to speak. At least no more anger is vented at the chauffeur of the vehicle than that which is released at the one who knocks down a child, a young person or a robust, adult male. And traffic here is far from fast, relatively speaking.

In the U.S.V.I and/or Venezuela, for example, on the other hand, where traffic congestions are the order of the day, where everyone rushes everywhere, the punishment for knocking down and elderly aged person is far greater than that for knocking down any other individual, or anything else for that matter. This difference in treatment is accounted for by the culture of the countries, which vary in the importance and sacrosanctity they attach to their aged.

Mention must also be made that in certain societies, notably those of the U.S.A and South Africa, race and class concepts, which are themselves culture – based, play a significant role in determining the treatment of the aged therein. Needless to mention, the poor and non- white elderly are given superficial, cursory, inefficient attention at best and no recognition whatsoever at worst. In the USA, for example, there is a much higher percentage of aged whites than blacks, yet a greater percentage of aged blacks are entirely homeless than whites. In South Africa, on the other hand, among the elderly, although at most ten percent is white, yet some ninety percent of the homeless ones are black.

These differing types of treatment of aged people certainly have far reaching implications for all who become aged in various societies.

For those who know that when they retire from active service, there is a comfortable home for them, there is an incentive to be industrious and consistent. They grow old in grace and live out their agedness in satisfaction. They are approached and consulted for advice and are looked upon as models to be emulated. For those, the culture of whose society treats them with scorn and disdain, and acts as though they become useless trash, they resign themselves to their fate and can only await the day of death, some of them wishing that it would hasten. Their progeny has no time for their companionship or admonition, and they regret ever having grown old. They curse the day they were born; hate the process of aging.

For the aged in societies like St. Kitts, the temptation is to resist agedness as soon as possible and hide its arrival by dressing like younger people, doing things (dancing, sports, etc.) like them, and painting the face to hide wrinkles, etc. They do not exert their influence or presence. They become secluded and solitary, and except for perhaps a few close relatives, they die in obscurity.

Other old people, in cultures that harbour racism and discrimination, they hate the system which tolerates these injustices and may urge others to rebel against it.

Almost all of them, however, because they retain their own values and, beliefs and customs and are reluctant and unable to accept change; because their offspring refuse to accept and practise their lifestyle; because they are sometimes forced to change(which means unwilling cooperation), there often results a generation gap, which if it is to be bridged, - and I propose that it must be bridged - , must be looked at and analyzed by those who are not yet 'old', with a view to stopping it when they become aged.

For no matter what is the culture base of their society, the aged therein, be they now or will be later, desire and no doubt deserve to live in harmony and peace and comfort with their younger coevals.

AN ARGUMENT FOR CAPITAL PUNISHMENT

Another murder. When shall the killings stop? The unpalatable fact of the matter is that St. Kitts – Nevis, with a population of approximately 45,000 persons, and with murders averaging 30 per year, has come to be one of the most violent and murder – prone societies on the planet earth. Some may wish to mount an argument that the problem is really not as serious as the statistics may suggest, given the probability that much of these killings may be drug – and gang driven.

But, in my humble estimation, the very serious issue is that causes of these homicidal acts notwithstanding, if the level of their incidence persists (far worse if it increases), it may well give rise to a sickening social acceptance of such internecine behavior as normal, and even expected, as one's sensitivity to and sense of umbrage at these murders become numb and inured overtime. This, I submit, only begets more violence, more murder. In fact, homicides might just become the order of the day.

I also contend that there is a suffocating anger at these killings that runs the gamut of social strata, some of it bred by despair arising from a sense of helplessness, perhaps even hopelessness, underpinned by a real or perceived inability to do something about it. There is, in addition, the incomprehensible reality of a deafening silence on the deadly trend on the part of the business, and, perhaps more importantly, the religious community.

I insist that this society in particular, given its miniscule size (nowhere to run for escape or shelter), cannot permit itself to go easy on or exercise any semblance of leniency towards those bent on killing, those found guilty of murder.

I propose that we hang the culprits as a matter of course. Let those who claim to be champions of 'human rights' damn to their hearts content. For there is ample evidence that an emphasis on 'human rights' has contributed directly to an abundance of human wrongs.

A 'life sentence' almost always translates into the culprit being housed, fed, entertained and protected by the State, using, of course , funds, monies and resources contributed by peace – loving, law abiding citizens and residents, including, so very unfairly, those of the family members and relatives of the victim.

A never – ending discussion as to whether capital punishment deters crime is, to me, pellucidly immaterial to this debate. I do not for one moment advocate an immediate resumption, or perhaps commencement of regular hangings of murderers premised on its deterrent effect.

Clearly, irrefutably, one thing is certain: hanging the murderer deters him/her from killing again, permanently.

Capital punishment, then, is retributive justice, pure and simple. Murderers must stew in their own grease. They must sow what they reap. For whosoever sheddeth man's blood, by man must his blood be shed.

I am convinced that because the penalty that murderers exact for their irreversible crime is neither swift, severe, nor sure, the rate of homicides continues apace.

Let us return to the gallows as a means of declaring that we are deadly serious about stemming the tide of murders that already threatens to wreak irreparable damage to our social, economic and political infrastructure and to upset our social equilibrium.

Hang them high!!!!

Must God Save the Queen in St. Kitts?

Britain's Queen Elizabeth II is St. Kitts' Head of State, and her royal profile graces the official currency. Our Police Force, 'Royal' as it is, enlists new members only after they have sworn allegiance to this monarch, and our prison, if names mean anything, is Her Majesty's domain. Of course, some persons are also incarcerated there 'at the Queen's pleasure'.

One of the highest paid and least -worked public officials purports to represent the Queen here, and according to the protocol hierarchy of prominence in this country, this agent of the sovereign is first amid 'equals'. The royal salute that military, police and para-military forces are trained to effect with smart and efficient precision is applied only for the monarch or her 'representative'.

"God, save the Queen", we sing. But should He? The Queen is, of course, the Queen of England, but is she really also the Queen of St. Kitts? How so?

It is an arguable proposition that the crown, the Queen, the monarchy, are psychological realities from which we derive a sense of order, permanence and belonging. It is wrong and misguided and dangerous to break with the tradition of pleading for God to save the Queen in St. Kitts, some say. After all, since 1783, when the Treaty of Versailles saw the French finally and fully cede 'Liamuiga' to the British (perhaps it is more correctly since 1623, when Thomas Warner landed here and set up house in the name of the then King), the monarch has not only been saved, he/she has been secure and sound.

There are those , Rastas included, who would suggests that we pledge our allegiance to a sovereign of Africa, if to anyone, while others, such as Jehovah's Witnesses, argue that it is best we swear to no one.

(This article, by the way, is not an argument for St. Kitts to become a republic, and all that entails. In fact, it is admitted that we might be better off beseeching God to save the Queen than we would fare having an 'Executive President' reign and rule over us. Rather, this seeks to provoke debate as to whether the symbolism that the Queen represents is worth preserving. Whether the pomp and ceremony – and expense – that accompanies the Sovereign's (or her representatives') visits to our shores are justified, especially in light of the fact that , generally speaking , the Queen herself is among the world's richest persons, perhaps its wealthiest woman, while many of her 'subjects' here and abroad endure an abiding, dehumanizing poverty. Also, it is no secret that Blacks et al in Her Majesty's native land experience racism in various forms as a fact of life, and that the Queen displays as much interest in us and our welfare as the Dalai Lama does in our big toe.)

The question is brief and blunt: what benefits, real or perceived, are derived from God's saving the Queen in St. Kitts? To repeat "Ut incepit fidelis" (Loyal it began, loyal it remains) is hollow and insufficient. Actually, I'd rather chant: "God, save the people!"

"To experience the full value of joy, one must have someone to share it with."

NATIONAL ASSOCIATION OF ADMINISTRATIVE PROFESSIONALS OF ST. KITTS AND NEVIS ANNUAL DINNER

'SURVIVING THE CHALLENGES'

Permit me to begin this address by admitting the extreme delight that envelopes me at being able to respond in the affirmative to your Association's kind invitation to be a part of your august body's week, which, I understand, runs from the 18th – 24th instant.

I wish also, from the onset, to congratulate and applaud the NAAP, St. Kitts Chapter, for its hitherto sterling record in championing the cause of Administrative Professionals in the country, while simultaneously calling your members to rise to the lofty heights of excellence and example in the discharge of your mandate.

Your organization is one of but a few bodies of professionals which are vibrant and visible, making a tangible, palpable contribution to the development and efficacy of the workplace, presenting yourselves as paragons of dedication and efficiency, constantly engaged in crafting strategies for individuals', corporate and collective advancement, and offering a service utterly indispensible for the smooth , effective operation of a multiplicity of businesses, firms, companies, sole entrepreneurs, and others whose success relates directly to the quality of expertise and service you singularly provide.

Clearly, your work, your duties, your tasks are critical to the survival of many, even most, if not all established offices.

And it is just as clear, just as true to aver that the high standard and quality outputs you set and generate do not emerge just like that. Yours is not at all a bed of roses, so to speak.

I feel free to declare with no need for explanation or fear of contradiction that you, as administrative professionals, experience trying times, difficult times, distressing times. I am fully aware that you confront many challenges, some regularly, some intractable, some unwarranted; but being the dedicated, trained, positive-minded-workers and professionals that you are, you devise, design and employ means by which to survive the challenges.

From all reports and observances, you adopt the maxim that challenges are to be faced, not shirked, and that the greater the challenge, the sweeter its overcoming.

You have learnt, from all appearances, to convert challenges to opportunities, and to translate difficulties into teaching and learning moments.

Let me remind you that when obstacles are piled high and you climb over them, you have ascended higher than you probably would have without them. Challenges are nature's way of developing strength.

Challenges, as Charles Spurgeon so aptly reminds us, encourage humility, urge inventiveness, build resilience, summon unknown, untapped powers, teach self reliance, generate collegial collaboration and , in the final analysis, develop character and bring grandeur to life.

And, so, I wish to encourage you to see challenges as blessings in disguise, especially since the Almighty Creator Himself, the very best exemplar of a professional, promises that He will not permit to come your way, our way, any challenges that are too much for us to bear.

But then, really, what are some of the challenges that perhaps are peculiar to Administrative Professionals?

I dare opine that such a list would include the following:
Office automation, with its threat, or, at the very least potential of making some jobs redundant and/or obsolete, thus threatening your livelihoods.

The constant need for change and/or upgrade of skills on an ongoing basis. Most pronouncedly, I am certain, is the demand for you to be on the cutting edge of technology, up - to-date and conversant with the latest trends and developments in administrative innovations.

The demand for greater output in the workplace, sometimes without the requisite or commensurate wherewithal.

An increasingly more demanding and challenging public, more sophisticated clientele, and a more discriminatory customer base.

Keeping au fait with the alacrity and velocity of changes in information technology, familiarity with and competence in which is a 'sine qua non' for administrative professionals in these modern times.

Adjusting to the expanding role of the administrative professional.

Frequent lack of adequate equipment, storage, and/or easy retrieval of information etc...

Coping with and adjusting to the issue of insufficient recognition and/or acknowledgement of the worth and the value of the administrative professional, contributing to mediocre rewards and benefits, which generally, you often do not deserve.

Being the human, social and civil face of your workplace; being the critical link between the client and your supervisor or boss.

The foregoing, I am sure, represents but a synopsis of the issues and challenges that you confront as a matter of course in your line of work. It is certainly not presented as an exhaustive list of that which calls for your best skills in compromise, creativity, patience, tact, frugality and adaptability.

But I must remind you by reiterating the fact that the history of mankind, the record of civilization speak eloquently of man – and woman's – demonstrating versatility and tenacity by facing and surmounting tremendous challenges over time.

In fact, we are well aware of the inevitability of challenges in the human experience. Life itself is a challenge, it is well said. But for life, including life as an administrative professional, to be meaningful, full, rewarding and successful, I submit that the real and ultimate challenge is to craft and share techniques, strategies and mechanisms to survive, to overcome, to triumph.

I recommend, as Phillip James Bailey does in 'Living Life', that you do more than move, you improve; do more than look, you must see; do more than sympathize, help; do more than agree, cooperate; do more than survive, conquer; do more than live, love.

I challenge you to continue to love, since it is the panacea to all ills, and it is indisputably the best answer and route to meeting challenges.

Love your work; love your family; love your country; love your life; love yourself, love your fellowmen; love God.

Ralph Waldo Emerson puts it nicely when he submits that every challenge presents an opportunity to acquire strength and virtue. You are bigger and greater than any challenge you may face. This self-discovery provides an insight that can go far in empowering you to go beyond mere survival.

Machiavelli himself it was who exhorts that where the willingness is great, the challenges cannot be greater.
I close by encouraging you to adopt the mantle of the brave, the positive, the optimist, the over – comer: "Come when you will, trial and challenge; nature's and my powers of discipline and refinement are polished and appointed: I am ready!"

Congratulations again and may God bless you and us all bountifully throughout this, your week, and beyond.

"Man himself creates the evil he endures."

Our Duty To Our Young People

Society tends to pounce with glee upon any occasion or incident in which a young person excels, or even does well, or appears to do so.

This no doubt is due to the fact that such an occurrence is a rare but welcome moment in time, a refreshing relief from the ordinary, the typical, which is characterized by a general plenteousness of idleness and indecency and an abundance of selfishness, aggression and mediocrity.

It not unfair or inaccurate to posit that in general, young people seem far more caught up with the unbridled worship of the gods of music, sex, sports and glamour than with the more noble duty of being models, exemplars and beacons of industry, ambition and rectitude.

Even an exiguous or cursory observation would reveal tellingly that the mode of dress, speech and choices reflects tastes and values that are essentially inimical to intellectual, social, moral and spiritual growth and acumen.

And so we are more than delighted when one or more of our youngsters achieve beyond the average or display qualities superior to the typical. We wish and long for many more instances of youthful wholesome, socially – pleasing developments.

But the truth is that many, easily too many youths today have no concrete conception of social responsibility, no fundamental appreciation of the value of education, no more than a hardly-discernible iota of compassion for life, and very little concern about loyalty, charity or chivalry. (Ask our teenage girls about their view of virginity and chastity, for example, and be prepared!)

Why is this so? Why are the young people so obviously morally bankrupt, intellectually bereft, and socially irresponsible? Why are they, by and large, so profoundly spiritually disconnected? Why is their moral compass, moral sense organ, moral conscience, so seriously dysfunctional?

Certainly we cannot deny the significant lack of parental guidance, or role modeling from those in 'authority', including teachers, ministers of government, ministers of religion, police officers, so-called youth leaders, and other adults in society at large.

Of course, none can outrank the supreme role and responsibility of parents in this regard, with both mothers and fathers failing, often miserably, in their divinely-sanctioned duty t o rear and train children in the right way, including teaching by precept and practice the values of goodwill, brotherly love, inclusiveness, honesty, patience, tolerance gratitude and forgiveness, among others.

But others of us are substantially guilty, by acts of omission and commission, of creating the conditions now punctuated so acutely by youthful waywardness.

And what a shame this is! Are we truly aware of the extent of the mental potency, physical strength and creative potential of young people?

Is our behaviour in the education sphere, the political arena and religious circles helping or hindering movement upward, onward and forward?

The fact of the matter is that it is we the adults who are largely responsible for not blazing trails, creating paths and setting standards which our youths are to follow in a positive and progressive model.

More often than not, adults contribute heavily to the ongoing debasement of society, as we so glibly flaunt the most vulgar and explicit forms of social and moral decadence in our no-holds-barred quest for money, power and control.

Our entire culture is coarsened, our conscience seared, our manners brutish, and our conduct scatological. The collective impact on our youth is far from subtle, gradual, crude or infantile. For they tend to close their eyes to advice and open their eyes to example.

And yet, in spite of a clearly worsening socio-politico-economic state of affairs, we can only do our individual part in the struggle to relieve this sad reality by ensuring that our own conduct and behaviour reflect a genuine intention to reform and a commitment to leading by example.

Not only must we learn to live together as brothers, or perish separately as fools; we must recognize the veracity of the dictum that we cannot expect to live (in front of our young people) lives of conflict, disequilibrium, opprobrium and distaste, and expect the rising generation – our future! – to do differently.

"Speak not because you have to say something but rather because you have something to say."

"The objective of oratory is not truth, but persuasion."

PARENTS – THE MISSING DIMENSION

Sir Francis Bacon, in an instance of unassailable wisdom, once posited that "Knowledge is power." Indisputably, the esteemed Englishman is right. However, whether that power is employed for purposes good or evil is an altogether different matter, for in this the most advanced of any society to inhabit the Blue Planet, violence, immorality and greed abound in unprecedented proportions, even as knowledge ebbs and flows.

Indeed, when the late Soviet dictator Joseph Stalin declared with passion in 1950 that "education is a weapon, whose effect depends on who holds it and at whom it is aimed", he was vociferating a profound truth: education - or the lack of it - shapes and dictates our outlook, behaviour and lifestyle.

But more importantly, and more relevant to this debate, is the necessity, the paramount importance of not merely passing knowledge to the young, but more so educating these rising multitudes in the proper disciplines and in the right direction.

The lamented Greek philosopher Aristotle consummates this truism when he admonishes: "The fate of empires (and nations) depends on the education of the youth."

It is to me puerile and futile to attempt to debate the merits and demerits of the (quantity and quality of) education that the young receive at school today. Suffice it to say that much money, time and effort are extended year after year in an endeavour to produce a literate and well- rounded youth, but again and again, we are disappointed by the product, as concretized by the attitudes, skills and general intellectual disposition of our students.

And I hereby suggest – nay – I submit that there is a missing dimension to this exercise of educating the youth, a crucial but absent ingredient in the recipe for success in this direction: parents.

Dare any honest parent or guardian contest the proposition that education begins at the mother's knee, and that what is said and done in the home tends toward the formation of character moreso than in any other setting, including, of course, the school? That men are what their mothers' make them needs neither defense nor explanation.

Alice Hawthorne's poem "What is home without a mother?" begs an answer. Michael S. Blake – Esdaille adds for the record that without parents' support, input and participation, the process of education is rendered sterile, woefully one-sided, and incomplete.

Simply and bluntly, far too many parents are content to dump their problems and their children on the schools, expecting, naively and vainly, the education system, with all its weaknesses and overburdened teachers, to absolve them of their God – given responsibilities.

Parents must not only know that a child educated only at school is an uneducated child, but that education is not necessarily if at all synonymous with academic proficiency or technical ability. They must be aware that education is not an end in itself, but as a means to an end; that which facilitates the realization of certain goals and objectives.

I call on parents, without distinction to race, class, sex, age, intellectual levels or status, to recognize, as the U.S Secretary of Education reminds us, that…. "not all teachers are parents, but all parents are indispensable as teachers."

Think of yourselves as the missing element in this whole panorama. Come to grasp with the challenge that is inherently yours to support and assist in your child's total development. Alleviate the demands on teachers by instilling indelibly, a sense of discipline, industry and cooperation in your children, ever conscious of the fact that children often close their ears to advice, but always open their eyes to example.

Like teachers everywhere, parents must believe that education, like charity, begins at home.

Ruin Unto Mankind

The story is told of a preacher who ended his sermon by saying that liquor was such a problem in the country that if he had his way, he would take all the rum in the land and throw it into the river. He then went on to ask for a member to choose a closing song, whereupon an old man got up and loudly suggested; "Shall we gather at the river?"

This might sound humorous, but it amply demonstrates the extent to which some persons, and especially geriatrics and older people, love and are addicted to rum. It proves decisively, that alcoholism is indeed a social problem in our country.

Despite the charges that have been brought against it, rum has continued to enjoy preference to and dominance over other drinks, and now, inspite of the dangerous effects that even its "moderate" use produces, many persons have an irresistible desire for 'a drink.' Consequently, dipsomaniacs abound everywhere, and it is nauseating to observe so many, especially older persons lying at the side of the road, sometimes in drains, with their private parts exposed and mumbling some inarticulate garble.

Alcohol no longer holds a reputation for excellent medicinal value, as it did in the past, for in this century, one has seen emerge with frightening, unprecedented proportions, the social, physical and mental damage of this drug. Rum consumption has now become a major phenomenon and a social problem in the Western World.

We have been so accustomed to seeing men and women become stupid and absent – minded from inebriety that we are now complacent and unconcerned. But drunkenness, more often than not, makes a family break up faster and results in workers' absence from work, lateness for work, or sluggishness at work. Such a situation, is, of course, counter – productive to economic growth. Furthermore, in a permissive society such as ours, the frequent abuse of liquor renders it more despicable.

Indeed, the effects and damage of rum has long been defined as unpalatable. Many crimes (and accidents) are committed by men under the influence of alcohol, and needless to say, any drink that ultimately renders its consumers unable to act properly and orderly, any beverage which causes its drinkers to act in anti-social ways is obviously a social evil and is therefore undesirable.

Rum is such a drink, and should therefore be kept in check, if not (preferably) totally gotten rid of. After all, we all do definitely detest and do not want anything that produces or represents the slightest resemblance of Ruin Unto Man.

"Some people love work. It fascinates them. They can sit and look at it for hours!"

"Anyone who stops learning is old, whether he be twenty or eighty."

Salvation Army Pre-school Graduation
8ᵗʰ July 1999
Theme: One Step at a Time

A journey of a thousand miles begins with one step. The greatest distances, just as the shortest, are covered, accomplished, completed one step at a time.

Steps are therefore important. If we do not take them, we get nowhere. We remain static, like statues, become stagnant.

Even to gain entrance into our homes, workplaces, schools, places of worship, entertainment, you name it, we use steps. And we use them one step at a time.

This is very important. For yes, steps are critical, indispensable, if you please, for us to move upward, onward and forward. But no matter how many steps there are, we must take them, not all at once, but one at a time.

This is so for the good of our health, physical agility and mental comfort.

Just as we ask God to help us take and live one day at a time, so we must implore Him to assist us in taking one step at a time.

You see, when we operate on the principle and adopt the practice of progressing one step at a time, we are able to maintain more effective control of our actions, and it facilitates more efficient use of our time, energies and resources.

One step at a time enables us to remain focused on the goal we have set for ourselves and our children. Our children, of course: these precious little boys and girls here with us this evening.

How we love them! Some of us adore them. Some, no doubt, idolize and worship them. I must hope that none of us abuses them. But, of course, I need not emphasize that in order to be successful, model parents and guardians, we must deal with them one step at a time.

As these dearly-beloved children, who are so utterly dependent on others, especially adults, for their safety, protection, growth and development, as they go through the various stages of life – birth, babyhood, infancy, toddlerhood, kindergarten, etc we must remember that these stages occur not in leaps and bounds, but surely consecutively, if you please, one step at a time.

So we as parents and guardians must ever use tolerance, patience, kindness, compassion, understanding and support with these our well-loved, cherished offspring.

Too often, in our times, we encourage, tolerate and practise instant gratification. We want things now, and we want them all now.

If your child is, in our eyes, somewhat slow in shaping his letters, spelling his name, counting his numbers, if he is not learning or demonstrating a learning of them fast enough for us, we tend to get upset, concerned and out-of-control. What we ought to do instead is remember the child has to learn and proceed one step at a time. Some steps might to be bigger than others, but it's one step at a time, all the same.

In general terms, by and large, people today do not want to take one step at a time. Too many of our fellow human beings want to jump several steps at a time, in order to get there fast, to get there first.

And, of course, we pass on these habits and behaviours to our innocent, susceptible children. The result, sadly, is that generation after generation display attitude of selfishness, individualism and impatience. They cannot bother with taking one step at a time.

Again and again, people hurt themselves and others, including their very own children and children of others, in the attempt to take several, sometimes even all steps at a time.

On this auspicious ascension of the Salvation Army School Graduation Ceremony for 1999, I appeal to the teachers and helpers of this institution, to help the students, the children here, to take one step at a time.

They learn to listen, speak, read and write in stages, they develop the various sensory motor skills one at a time. And so, even as I congratulate special children who are graduating from the school this evening, I must simultaneously express thanks, appreciation and congratulations to you the parents, the Major, assistants, for recognizing the importance of dealing with the children of this school one day at a time, one step at a time.

The Bible injuncts that charity suffereth long. Voltaire once said that any journey worth undertaking, must be done meticulously and in steps, and I myself this evening ask of you, of all of us, that we take these precious, special, cherished children into our care and lead them by the hand into the 21st century, and indeed, into the kingdom of God, one day, one step at a time. Thank you.

"Given how hard it is to change ourselves, no wonder it is so difficult to change others."

"People who get carried away by their own rhetoric should be."

Start of SKTU's Teacher's Week 2015

Fellow citizens, brothers, sisters, residents, ladies, gentlemen, students, teachers, all.

I am pleased to bid a cordial welcome and good evening to each of you listening and looking at this time to this our national radio and television, ZIZ.

I am here on this occasion to address you, not for an unduly long time, on the matter of the celebration of Teachers Week, which this year runs from October 3rd through to next Saturday 10th instant.

I wish to begin my discourse with you by saluting all teachers, everywhere. I greet all those involved and engaged in this noble profession, with a profound and overriding sense of pride, gratitude and appreciation.

Yours is a contribution unmatched, and I dare say, unmatchable, anywhere on the planet.

I wish to extend to you on behalf of the Ministry of Education, and on my behalf, very best wishes for a school/academic year, already almost one month old, which will be free of danger or distress, and which will bring to you, your profession, your colleagues, your schools, your students, your families, your union, and your country, untold, unprecedented growth, prosperity, development and success.

And I dare propose that government, my government, has already contributed in a tangible way toward facilitating the realization of this objective of achieving excellence in all areas of your operation as teachers by ensuring that all schools are as fully staffed as possible, that there is an adequacy of needed supplies, and that the students at the Basseterre High School are just about to enter their new temporary building at Taylors, which of course, will significantly improve their level of comfort and their teaching and learning experience.

But I want now to again congratulate and thank you teachers, you facilitators of learning, for your persistent and characteristic hard work over the years, including, of course, the one just past.

The Ministry is satisfied that by and large, the teaching fraternity in St. Kitts and in Nevis, is one of quality. Because it is abundantly clear to me that it takes teachers of exceptionally high caliber, operating at an elevated standard, to produce the kind of results in our students, as you have.

You teachers have defied the odds, and have achieved remarkable feats. For despite facing several problems in the modus operandi of your profession, in spite of the lack of sometimes critical resources in expertise, material and amenities, you produce results that tend to get better year after year.
Indeed, it is apt to say that you have achieved much without much, and congratulations are certainly in full order.

We in Government, Team Unity, are committed to working to expedite the process designed to ensure that working conditions for all teachers are improved to the best state possible, as a tangible means of demonstrating how much we honour and value you and your work.

But I must continue now by reiterating the extreme confidence that I, as Minister of Education, have in you, faithful, reliable, committed members of the profession, devoted to the task of providing quality education to our rising generation.

This confidence I repose in you teachers, is derived from your very commendable performance over the past academic year, strengthened and supported, as it were, by previous instances of sterling performances by you year after year.

The outstanding results of our students at the Test-of Standards, CXC and CAPE exams is irrefutable testimony of the strength and quality of your input in the teaching – learning process, and so on this the start of Teachers Week 2015, I salute you, again. I also salute you, the nation's teachers, not just as member of the Teachers' Union, which is in and of itself a very useful, desirable and welcome fact and reality, but even more so as practitioners of a common fraternity called teaching.

It is the collective effort of individuals such as yourselves which is largely if not exclusively responsible for creating an environment in which we can boast that the standard of education in our Federation is as good as many and better than most.

Teachers, let there be no doubt about it. It is you, in the judicious, intelligent discharge of your duties as teachers, who are the reason, the cause of the fact that the education system on St. Kitts is making strides.

For this, I wish to thank you most profoundly and genuinely. And in recognition of the outstanding contribution of one of our recently-fallen comrade-in-arms, so to speak, I ask now that you join me in observing one minute's silence in respect and remembrance of our late sister teacher, Mrs. Yvonne Walters, better and affectionately as Teacher Mulley, who died just last week. She has been a teacher for an aggregate of almost 40 years. Thank you. May her soul ever rest in peace.

And now, for those of you left on the land of the living, still occupying residence on God's planet earth, the challenge is yours to commit yourselves to ensure that you do all in your poser to so employ your talents, resources and efforts that you create the most comfortable environment for your students, so that their learning could be better, faster, wider and deeper.

I agree with the former Hon. Minister of Education, Sam Condor, when he advised that if one does not have the best conditions to work in or under, he must nevertheless make the best of whatever conditions prevail.

I really think that this is sound advice, because the reality in that given the nation's limited resources, it may not be possible to always have the very best.

Of course, this is not to say that we must not argue for the better. Most certainly not. After all, not only is room for improvement never full, but your very motto obliges and expects you to 'agitate, educate, liberate'.

So you will ever be in the vanguard of the movement for improved educational outputs from your clients, the students. There is no need to stress the point that better teaching conditions for all workers, including teachers, lead to better learning conditions for our students, and this would surely itself lead to better behaviour from, more pleasant attitudes of , and greater performance by our students.

Always remember that the interest of your students is your main focus. Your students' welfare and well-being, academically, morally, and otherwise, must always be your central concern.

I wish also to use this occasion to plead with you teachers to recommit yourselves to working towards a better, more successful, productive, academic year 2015-2016.

We must hear less complaints from your co-workers, your supervisors (principals and education officers), our parents, our students, our business sector and the wider community, about some teachers' unbecoming behaviour on and off the school compound. There are too many complaints, legitimate complaints I may add, of some of our teachers not preparing work, being regularly late and absent, being improperly and inappropriately attired, using less-than-decent language in the presence of students, not attending or participating in staff meetings, development sessions, extra-curriculum activity, etc., without proper reason or excuse.

May I remind you that not only is such a behaviour from and among teachers unprofessional and unacceptable, but also, it compromises the integrity of the profession, and weakens the position of SKTU when it has to make representation on your behalf, for whatever reason.

I plead with you to desist from such unpleasant behaviours. Even one instance from one teacher can permanently and seriously hinder our collective and/or individual progress.

Fortunately, such teachers who may be the subject of these complaints are in the clear minority.

Because, thankfully, the majority of our teachers are honest, dedicated, and, as such, are very much appreciated and honoured.

Indeed, page 21 of our own 'road map' for education, the White Paper on Education Development and Policy 2009 – 2019, reiterates that (quote) "Teachers work is valuable and indispensable" (end quote).

Yet I firmly hold that in order for teachers and teaching to be truly worthy of the accolade long ago bestowed on it by the Roman Statesman Cicero as being the most noble of professions, we must together cleanse and refine the chambers of the imagery of our teachers by translating criticism into assistance. The sages and heroes of History may be receding from us, and our contemporaries may contract the records of our deeds in a narrower page, but a bright and fair future beckons to behold and to be held if teachers are honoured as ought.

This week, Teacher's Week 2015, is to be one of the sober reflection and introspection. It must also be an occasion for celebration.

I wish to conclude by repeating my love and respect for the teaching profession, and my confidence in you teachers to deliver a quality product. Let us re-dedicate ourselves to the principle that teaching is a profession too noble and too indispensable for mediocrity and lassitude. It calls you to a high and lofty plane.

May we rise majestically to the occasion. And it is anticipation and expectation that our teachers in the federation will so rise, that I hereby declare open the St. Kitts Teachers Union Teachers Week 2015.

I wish it complete success.

The Case for Reading

A catastrophe of horrendous proportions on an unprecedented scale is brewing, portending the worst of times. It is a matter of national import and impact that has serious implications for individuals, families, business, civil society, government, diplomacy, and, indeed, all areas of human activity. It is a problem with / of READING.

A majority of persons, from all appearances, do not read, pure and simple. And they do not read because they CANNOT read. Nor do they not read due to a paucity of reading material. Literary / printed works abound in the presence of a smorgasbord of magazines, books, newspapers, the internet, et al, which severally and together, offer a content variety that caters to every conceivable reading taste. Rather, they do not read because they have no interest, pure and simple. And, of course, again and again, we are pelted with the statistic that ours is a society that boasts a 98% literacy rate. (Yes, statistics are one of the three ways to tell/spread inveracities.) What a contradiction!

But it is patently the case that reading no longer is pursued as a matter of course or a matter of fact among/by a large majority of our students (so-called 'studying' and cramming, using subject text books for the purpose of 'passing' an exam definitely does not count as Reading!)

This culture of non – reading is growing far and wide, fast and furious (no thanks to the ubiquity of cellular / iphones, etc.) , and threatens, in both the short and long terms, to suffocate efforts at individual, institutional and national development, and to confine us to the pavilion of spectators as the world moves inexorably to higher levels of advancement in science, technology, and economic development. For make no bones about it, the movers and shakers of the world, those who own and control the commanding heights of the global economy, those who MAKE things happen, they read, and read a lot!

That persons do not read, or more certainly, do not read widely or sufficiently, is manifested, among other ways, in the content (or lack thereof) of their speech; quality of their conversations / oral intercourse; contribution to public/ open debates, discussions, etc.; quick resort to foul, vulgar language; ignorance of world affairs; tendency to be mere mimic men, as opposed to being original, critical thinkers; dearth of knowledge of latest trends in education, health/medicine, etc.; rabid aversions to buying books, either hard copies or electronic versions; and, very tellingly, what and how they write! Students in particular demonstrate a frightening avoidance of Reading via the dismally-poor 'quality' of their writing and speaking outputs (content, logic, diction, syntax, grammar, spelling, etc). Far, far too often, whether they be in 'lower' primary or 'upper' secondary or beyond, their writing is tantamount to glib butchery of the language.

Francis Bacon contends that Reading maketh a full man. Addison posits that Reading is to the mind what exercise is to the body. Yet it is a rather difficult challenge to convince others, students and adults alike, of the importance, nay the necessity of Reading.

As humans, we are, naturally, constantly looking for the meaning of life. In that search, Reading plays a key role. And this is critical indeed, because man's obsession with/near worship of entertainment (particularly music and sports), sex, money, and power would be constructively served and effectively moderated if he were to engage in deep, intentional reading on these issues, including their many merits and demerits.

But besides this very real and mundane predisposing factor, we, people, young and not-so-young alike, should read for pleasure, for personal growth, as an escape, not from reality, but to realms of imagination and virtual ecstasy, for information, to develop creativity, to stretch the mind (and of course, a mind, once stretched, never returns to its original dimensions!), to build/ improve vocabulary, to enhance writing skills, to share the experiences, ideas and ideals of others, to glean and enhance writing styles, and for both individual and collective enrichment. Books, for one, after all, provide relief from idleness, rescue from bad company, comfort of good company, balm for loneliness, and a means of blunting the edge of grief.

Reading facilitates more and better social interaction, imbuing one with self – assurance and self-esteem to participate meaningfully in the (decent) conversations of the day. Works presenting History, Philosophy, Religion, Science, personal stories, biographical narratives and national experiences, via poetry and prose, open our eyes and minds, and transport us to lands and heights of both spiritual and temporal pleasure, growth and satisfaction.

Active Reading constitutes a social dialogue between reader and author, and often, the target and purpose of the writing find resonance, residence and completion in the reader, leading the latter to create solutions to problems and reasons to engage in moment of quiet, introspective reflection.

Of course, if truth be told, not all published material, on paper or on screen, is worthy of being read. The content, the intent and vocabulary of some writings are wholly indecent, harmful and negative to individual, social and public morality. Many publications indeed, far from being tomes, edifying or positive, are markedly degrading and/ or deliberately mis-informative, not worth the paper they are printed on.

This means that one should be discriminatory and selective in the things he reads or chooses to read. Fortunately, a plentitude of books, magazines, etc., which presents that which is constructive, wholesome, stimulating, esthetic and sublime, exists ubiquitously.

Reading ought to be a thoughtful, interactive, intellectual, pleasant activity, not a hurried, light, mechanical, superficial exercise. It should focus on quality, not the number of pieces read.

Notwithstanding the cursoriness of some persons' reading, it can never be gainsaid that Reading is the carrier of civilization. Without it, history is silent, science is crippled, thought and imagination stand still, and, of course, literature is dumb. Reading is an engine of change, a window of and to the world, and a light house amidst a sea of mental darkness. And yet, no entertainment is so cheap, no pleasure is as lasting as reading.

The Bible, for example, is inarguably the most influential book, or set of books, ever written. It presents History, knowledge, wisdom, advice, warning, promises, prophecies, hope and spiritual empowering in both poetic and essay-style genres with glowing beauty, in sublime and solemn majesty, in touching pathos; exacting a response, exuding an authority and effecting (strictly positive) change in its readers of a kind and in a way that no opus, past, contemporary or yet to come, has ever replicated or can ever emulate.

When / if people read, they can learn anything. Books, etc, are doors that open the world to those who read. And in this connection, it is supremely important that reading be shared with and instilled in our young children at a very early age. It is now long settled that Reading for/to youngsters helps them develop their sense of hearing and vision, contributes to their language development, increases their learning ability, stimulates their capacity to distinguish sounds, facilitates the process of reading, strengthens the developing brain, broadens the knowledge base, encourages the habit of studying, engenders more confidence in/and about themselves, cultivates a useful pastime, and develops their emotional and intellectual faculties, among other desirable benefits and advantages.

In our schools then, Reading must be taught to and mastered by our students as a sine qua non for promotion to a higher level. A student who cannot read, or who cannot read well, who cannot perform well in any subject area, should be remediated, not punished or ostracized, if he lacks competence in Reading.

Far, far too many of our students of the day simply cannot read well, and they are not properly encouraged – or even helped – so to do. And automatically 'promoting' them to be the next (higher) grade definitely does not at all help!

The mere presence of books exudes comfort, their ready access, re-assurance. And the material of their construction makes them able to withstand falls and being tossed hither and thither. Of course, they can also live and last from generation to generation.

Clearly, indisputable, he who reads well and reads much, grows to speak well and write well, and has a distinct, palpable advantage over he who does not.

Moreover, he who does not read is worse/ worse off than he who CANNOT read.

Like Jorge Luis Borges, I might not be proud of what I wrote, but I am sure proud of what I read.
Let us READ!!!

"There are two types of education: one teaches us to make a living, the other, how to live."

"ANGER: just one letter short of DANGER."

The Glory of Our Culture

In the jargon of sociology, culture refers to all those elements and behaviours acquired by human beings which are not biologically inherited. Thus, by definition, our culture includes, inter alia, our music and its derivatives, our local dishes, our dialect, our political and social structures, our dress, our value system, tastes and religious predisposition, among others.

In my estimation, however, culture becomes unique, rich and meaningful only when all its various aspects, diverse yet interrelated, are used for the societal, economic, political, intellectual and aesthetic development of a community and the people resident therein.

Culture both assumes and bestows a characteristic of uniqueness and specificity to a country, for no two societies are alike, notwithstanding the fact that many may share similar historical experience, exhibit identical behavioural patterns, and construct and employ like social structures.

Our own culture must therefore be suited to our particular purpose, and nurtured to satisfy our needs and aspirations. It must be safeguarded and preserved as our exclusive domain, as it represents the only thing that we can bequeath to prosperity as genuinely and solely our own. As such, deliberate efforts must be undertaken to ensure that it is neither corrupted nor diluted.

But today, in contemporary sociological circles and beyond, the debates rages as to whether we in the developing world, and especially with a diaspora so very widely scattered, do have a legitimate claim to a culture.

At first resort, this might seem an insulting and ridiculous assertion. But, after scrutiny, is that not a fair question? Because, in truth, so very often, stripped of all its foreign content and reduced to its bare essentials, our (Caribbean) 'culture' leaves precious little that is genuinely indigenous to be desired.

I submit that, deliberately or subconsciously, we have allowed our culture, especially during recent times, to be contaminated by the influx and influences of external forces. And we have done very little if anything genuine or consistent to prevent or even mitigate the adulteration of our cultural forms and norms from the subtle, sometimes overt distortions of, specifically, American cultural penetration.

So that the glory of our culture is at stake. It is being erased, and replaced by a foreign content and substance which, by and large, is inimical to the realization of our goals and aspirations. This 'replacement' is a rotten substitute for what ought to be glorious and unique.

Of course we are eternally grateful for , appreciative of and consumed in delight by our masquerades, clowns, calypso, steel pan, conkies, goat water, dialect, architectural styles, and groups such as our drummers and dancers a la Okolo Tegremantine Theatre (congratulations to the OTDT on the occasion of their 40th anniversary!).

But even so, and even here, we find, too often for comfort, elements and ingredients in their contents and structure that are, at the very least, suspect as to the relevance thereof to our cultural uniqueness, heritage, enhancement and preservation.
And how many of the various aspects/dimensions of our culture are truly and wholly, or even substantially, home grown? How much of it is essentially a copy (sometimes crude and vulgar) of some other countries?

Certainly, we need our very own Cultural Centre, cultural policy, cultural practices, and cultural identity. And these must become a deliberate, conscious, living facet of our very being and our national psyche.

A clarion call is thus being issued to all those who, in some way or other, can be instrumental in reversing this trend towards us becoming purely "Mimic Men".

These include parents, educators, artistes, performers, and the media. We must rise to action now, in particular to confront the mass media, and challenge the clearly-less-than-wholesome content that it pours forth and encourages us, especially the young, to accept as good and imitable, and as culturally correct, culturally ours.

Simultaneously, let us explore literature, the very media (electronic and print) the open platform, discussions, seminars, the school and all other available for a in the absolutely crucial and now extremely urgent struggle to preserve the glory of our culture.

"If we made do with what we need rather than contest for what we want, we would be at peace."

"The most sublime and solemn responsibility of schools is to teach every child to read; if they do not accomplish this task, they have failed."

The Role Of The Modern Police Force

Like all institutions in society, the police force serves a clearly-defined purpose in the particular system of things, and not unlike any other organization that is comprised of men, the functions and performances of the Police have evolved over time.

Today, in the so-called 'modern age' of man's historical experience, the role of the Police is essentially the preservation of law and order in society, including, by definition, the detention of individuals or groups of individuals whose activities, by accident or design, present a credible threat to the societal state of affairs, threaten to upset the status quo, and are considered inimical to public safety, well-being or morality.

Such a demand, such an expectation, to my mind, lends urgency to the obligation of the Force to discharge its role without fear or favour, malice or ill will, and with consummate professional acumen.

In the final analysis, you see, evil is evil, regardless of who perpetrates it, and the committing of wrong has never been confined to the rulers or to the ruled.

Certainly a fundamental function of the Police is the prevention, detection and investigation of crime, and the pursuit and arrest of those involved in perpetrating acts contrary to the laws of the land. (It is very important to stress that trial and conviction is the domain of the Courts alone.)

But in no way can even the most autistic or nescient of minds limit the role of a modern Police force to these confines.

Let it be established that the police officer himself is not ever a special person immune from the ordinary process of the courts. He is not a law unto himself with absolute, unquestionable power and authority.

Most definitely, the Police constitutes an utterly indispensable entity in our scheme of things, for as society advances into the more complex and sophisticated, as the nature and extent of human inter-relationships fluctuate, and as crime and violence ebb and flow, without the Police, I submit that sooner than later, chaos, recklessness and fear would descend upon the land with horrifying, unprecedented consequences.

But in law, a policeman is merely a private citizen with a specific duty and specialized powers to keep the peace. Any abuse of this vested authority is a misuse of power, and disqualifies the errant one from being morally eligible to be charged with the responsibility of being a Police Officer.

It is my view that, in essence, the Police should represent, epitomize, represent and present Protection, Order, Law-enforcement, Intuition, Courage and Efficiency. This acrostic, in my humble estimation, adequately spells out the role of the Police in any modern society.

Naturally, the success, both quantitatively and qualitatively, of the Police depends on the caliber of the individuals of whom it is composed, which as one reason why eligibility for entrance therein must be premised on consistent, intelligently-thought-out criteria.

There must be excellent rapport between the rank and file of the Force. The relationship between the upper echelons and the lowest positions must be horizontal in structure and based on mutual trust and respect as they seek unity in pursuit of a common objective: Ensuring and maintaining the safety, security and protection of the citizenry – at – large and its property, is a paramount role and duty of the police.

There must be a conscious, deliberate and systematic attempt by the Police to cultivate harmonious relations with the public, whom it serves; to set before it a clear image of exemplary role models.

It is now merely platitudinous to reiterate that to a very large extent, the success – nay, the survival! – of the Police Force rests upon the cooperation it metes out to and receives from the general community.

The role of the modern Police Force, then, also includes its active involvement in all aspects of societal development, and this encompasses the erecting of physical structures, contributing to worthy community efforts, rendering expertise, security or vehicular assistance where requested, leading efforts of rescue and repair during/after natural and other disasters, and offering guidance, direction and support to the elderly, the helpless, the threatened.

Finally, it must be pointed out that since the Police Force is organized and paid for by the legally constituted government, it shares the duty of all civil servants to execute government policy. But this is not to be confused, substituted or adulterated with blind, Party- Political support, where its directives emanate from party bosses and are construed to militate against the interests and frustrate the legitimate demands of certain sections of society.

In other words, another and equal vital role of the Police Force is to be eternally vigilant and actively guard against any endeavour to transform and reduce it to an institution that pledges its allegiance to any particular single individual or political party.

"If you think education is expensive, try ignorance; if you think health is expensive, try sickness."

THE CASE FOR INTRODUCING 'PARENTING' EDUCATION IN SCHOOLS

Many persons are convinced – and statistics seem to buttress their belief – that the increasing and disconcerting palpable rise in incidences of robbery, burglary, wounding, shooting, killing and general violence is being perpetrated largely by young people, particularly males.

Sociologists have long established that it is violent crime, which by definition and practice always claims a victim, that citizens fear most, relative to other types of criminal acts.

This, of course, is quite understandable, as self-preservation is the first order of business, so to speak, first on the list of priorities for almost all of mankind. And violent crime, with its inherent threat to life and limb, directly opposes that superlative and supreme principle.

Violent crime often draws or threatens to draw blood, the essence of life. And the fact that each such act directly or indirectly, in one way or another, affects multiple individuals and families (given the realities of historically and culturally close kinship ties. No man is an island, after all.), means that in a very real sense, violent crime affects us all.

But it is not only violent crime that one must fear. In fact, violent crime is neither a cause nor an end in and of itself. Social Scientists unanimously agree that crime is a complex phenomenon whose causes and solutions are as manifold and intractable as any social problem, and more so than most.

Certainly, collective society must be altogether concerned about young people's general sociopathic behaviours, as manifested so readily, easily, pervasively and ubiquitously in repeated acts of disrespect (for self and others, including their person, reputation and property), aggression, impatience, indecency, foul language, immodest dress, inability to reason, lack of compassion, indolence, insolence, disregard for authority, and embrace of mediocrity, among other negatives. However, it is crime, violent crime, that obviously draws the most reaction and generates the most fear.

(Of course, I need not labour the FACT that very many, no doubt MOST of our young people, our young men, are NOT engaged in criminal activity!)

But since very much, in fact most of the serious 'blue-collar' crimes are apparently committed by 'misguided youths', many citizens / residents are quick to point the accusing finger at two major institutions in society, the Home and the School, as the breeding ground for these malevolents, and lay the blame for this malaise squarely at their feet. (The Church, too, is often accused of failing in its duty to help restrain youngsters from evil-doing.)

And perhaps they are right. The fact of the matter is that these crime-committers (persons generally ages 18 – 30) are, far more likely than not, simply outputting what they took in during their formative years (from birth to adolescence), when, of course, almost all of their daylight/ waking hours are spent at home and / or at school.

This means that parents and teachers failed miserably in their duty and responsibility to properly train, discipline, instruct and guide their children and students in a way that steers them away from being perpetrators and / or victims of crime in general, violent crime more so.

Further, it must be emphasized that notwithstanding the fact that most of the active daylight hours are sent at school for 36 or so weeks of the calendar year, it is a myth that is subscribed to by many that teachers and/or peers exert more influence on young people, particularly adolescents, than do their parents.

The truth is that field and action research, both in and beyond the region, has revealed, unambiguously, that it is the PARENT who still occupies that position, who exercises more/ most influence on students' behaviour, conduct and attitude.

If, then, we are to accept that young people acquire a propensity for violence during their development stages, then it stands to reason that parents carry the major portion of responsibly for their children, our young people's actions.

And this is one major reason why the need, the call for Parenting education in schools is clarion, clear, and compelling.

Parents are the first teachers that children know and meet, anyway. But parents, like others, cannot teach what they do not know. They cannot lead to where they do not go. And, by and large, they do NOT know how to properly and correctly parent a child. (Of course, some are definitely desirous of being good parents.)

The role of education as an institution is paramount in this scenario. My posit is that it is the formal school system and setting wherein the dynamics and details of parenting must be introduced, exposed, imparted.

Lamentably, the current generation of parents 'at fault' is difficult to reach in terms of effectuating the types of changes in parenting styles envisaged and desired. But for the sake of the future of society, to save upcoming generations, to see and enjoy a marked reduction in the myriad acts of wanton violence, cruelty, animosity, delinquency and other dehumanizing, inhuman acts being visited by man upon man, we ought to fitfully introduce Parenting as a discrete, core-curricula subject in our nation's schools, with immediacy.

Another major reason for such an innovation resides in the fact that whereas students, both males and females, upon exiting the formal school environment, will inevitably pursue a plethoric, eclectic multitude and variety of jobs/occupations/careers, it is simply inarguable that, realistically, upward of 90% of them will become PARENTS, some sooner than others, many several times over.

Clearly, something is patently amiss with a system that expands much time, energy, expertise, money and effort in preparing our students/young people for the world of adulthood which all (barring death) will attain, and for the world of work, which many will enter, but we do nothing or hardly anything deliberate, systematic, strategic or syngenetic to ready and prepare them for the role of parenthood, which most will assume.

Room can and must be found to accommodate Parenting in the curriculum. In any event, there already exists a crying need to revisit and reform the curriculum content to eliminate the duplication, redundancies and irrelevancies that suffocate it, and have it more meaningfully reflect and represent a set of learning experiences germane to the times.

Finally, I propose that Parenting education begin at Grade 3, and run the gamut until 5th Form, and that it includes in its instructional content the following emphases, inter alia: the social, spiritual, moral, physical, emotional and educational needs of children, and roles of parents in this respect; challenges and demands of single parenting; child development; kinship; protection and support of children; love vs. infatuation; virtues of chastity, abstinence and fidelity; competition; relationships; the manifold responsibilities of mothers and fathers; training and discipline of children; dangers of early sex and pregnancy; life chances; benefits of two-parent families; sanctity of marriage; costs of child rearing; role modelling; health issues; legal implications; culture, customs, norms, mores and values; and other relevant topics.

The crucial questions of WHO imparts this instruction, and the training requisite for them, are to be decided upon subsequent to the necessary sober, intense discussions and conversations attendant with this process.

But the potential for Parenting in schools to have constructive, positive effects on the outlook, behaviour, thinking and attitude of students, which will translate into better-behaved, more anti-sociopathic, less violent children and, by extension, a safer, more secure harmonious society, is immense and untapped. It begs for the dialogue to begin.

So let the discourse re Parenting in schools start in earnest. Now.

WHITHER CARNIVAL IN ST. KITTS?

An article in the recent local press, under the rubric 'Carnival and Morality' sought, sometimes abstrusely, I admit, to position Carnival and what it, in theory, ought to symbolize within the context of Society's manifestation of it, and to juxtapose it with morality.

The author(s) found, with reason, that current carnival activities, both in their intent, content and consequences, fall just shy of being diametrically opposed to even the slightest semblance of morality.

Certainly, the author is right. Contemporary celebrations of Carnival in St. Kitts seem, deliberately or in error, to take little note or have little knowledge of the origins and meaning of the event, and appear designed to appeal only to the baser instincts of man, to whet and satiate his appetite for revelry, and to provide license for him to engage in acts of excess and immorality with reckless abandon. The fact of the matter is that, Carnival, as currently constituted, operates in a vacuum of sorts, devoid of any real sense or understanding of what it even purports to be. What is packaged and presented as Carnival is a poor exercise in a 'festival of the flesh'.
Pathetically so.

Generally, here in the Caribbean, Carnival parades, for example, feature troupes for 100 or more persons, as a matter of course. Costumes and outfits are elaborate and extravagant in detail, and display an abundance of creative genius, imagination, skill and artistry. Some costumes occupy the entire width of a street at times, and troupes portray meaning and message in their design and display. Moreover, troupes and floats number in the dozens as a rule and practice.

In all of this, the emphasis is on displaying a lesson, propagating a message that, more often than not, has deep cultural, educational, scientific, political, religious or other type of significance, and is void of the plenteousness of immorality, vulgarity, obscenity, frivolity that have come to characterize our own local parade.

This New Year's Day's Carnival parade, for instance with its one- and – a – half troupe content, was decidedly shallow, to put it mildly. And year after year, a plethora of complaints and negative comments, some ludicrous and spiteful, most objective and legitimate, accompany the spectacle.

So that it seems pellucidly clear to me that Carnival in St. Kitts, particularly the parade, needs to be re – constituted as a matter of urgent national attention. Not only must the vulgar and sensual be reduced to their barest minimum, but also, and perhaps more importantly, the original meaning of the affair must be messaged.

I submit, therefore, that Carnival in SKB be de – politicized as a very first step towards its reconstruction. An excellent Carnival is not supposed to make the ruling party, whichever it is, 'look good', as a major objective or outcome. It must instead make the country look good. It must make the participants happy and safe, and make the multitude of spectators pleased and satisfied. Incumbent and opposing parties must actively sponsor, support and take part. This, coupled with de – emphasis on the crude and indecent behaviour displayed, is guaranteed to ensure massive, spontaneous participation and involvement of/by all strata of society, including the religious minded.

All this, however, will be counter – productive and ultimately self defeating if carnival in St. Kitts continues to be held in December, at Christmas time. Christmas and Carnival are incompatible, pure and total.

Carnival in December is anachronistic; a conundrum. For one, the demands of Christmas and of Carnival, coming as they do at the same time, strain the capacity of most to adequately meet them, both financially and logistically. No wonder there is so little participation in parade troupes.

Then, traditional folklore activities (masquerades, clowns, mock-jumbies, bull, etc) are subsumed by Carnival, which, of course, nevertheless does not sufficiently deliver.

And again of course, the sanctity and sobriety of Christmas are compromised, nay, adulterated, by the concurrent Carnival activities.

Carnival at another, more opportune and practical time therefore makes more sense, and cries out for serious attention, debate and consideration.

Thus, Christmas will regain and retain its sober prominence; folklore troupes will maintain their ascendancy on Boxing and New Year's Days, and one will b able to afford more time to plan and prepare for and more money to spend on both Christmas in December and Carnival in, let us say, late July/early August.

"To educate a man in mind and not in morals is to impose a menace on society."

"MIRTH CANNOT MOVE A SOUL IN AGONY."

A GRADE 'F' FOR THE CHURCH?

Does the Church achieve success in contemporary society? Does the Church's behaviour merit a performance grade other than an 'F'? These questions are both honest and urgent.

The age we inhabit at this juncture in our history and development is conspicuously characterized by a plenteousness of immorality and an abundance of evil. Men   - and women- engage unashamedly in acts of brutality and vice and wallow in a cesspool of greed and dishonesty with reckless abandon.

Men, women and children are both victims and perpetrators of hitherto unspeakable atrocities and indignities that are visited upon others without hesitancy or compunction. Clearly, now more than ever, compassion has fled to brutish beasts, and men have lost their reason.

Again and again, we hear of, read about, know of and/ or actually witness acts and actions that point and paint a dark and dismal picture of society, of mankind's sinking rapidly and ever deeper into an abyss of decay and decadence from which there seems to be no escape. Indeed, there seems to be no want to escape, even.

Where is the Church in this scenario? What is its role and duty? And is its mission, vision and modus operandi in our day germane to the times and equal to the task?

Many complain that the Church, via its actions, reactions, and/ or non-action, actually keeps its followers away from God, and does precious little to effect any meaningful or noticeable dent in the ungodly, unrelenting trends described above. The argument, indeed, is that, in a general sense, neither the Church nor its behaviour has produced a better society in all the 200 - plus years of its existence. Some say, in fact, that we profess to live in an age and ethnic of Christianity, yet our acts are as barbarous as though we never knew the Christ.

Here on St. Kitts, what is the Church's record with respect to proactive, pre - emptive stratagems and strategies to deal with rising levels of crime, violence, sexual deviance, immorality, injustice, inequality, poverty, abuse, political and business shenanigans, and wickedness in high places, among other ills? What is the Church's claim to fame as it pertains to interventions that lead people in general and young persons in particular to turn to Jesus Christ and change their lives for the better?

Apart from largely superficial and shallow 'invitations' to 'accept Christ'- made almost exclusively from within the confines of their places of worship, aided at times by the electronic media-, what is the Church's performance like? Does it approximate anything less than 'F'?

What, really and honestly, can the Church boast to have deposited in whatever repository of achievement it may possess, with respect to being viable, visible, audible and palpable in the struggle for social justice, for social cohesion, for peace, for love, for growth?

Indeed, the unpalatable fact but candid truth may very well be that the Church itself, not being at all a united entity nor a singular force, is bedeviled by internal isms and schisms that define and corrupt its body politic, and serve to continue to suffocate its ability to contribute significantly, or at least meaningfully, to not just the debate but, more importantly, to the strategy for action to and redress the manifold social, spiritual and other maladies that beset it, and us.

When the political directorate, school administrators, business moguls, the Courts, the security services, when these, separately or in combination, promulgate and pursue policies and programmes that are clearly inimical to the interests of a society professing adherence to a Judaea-Christian ethic, that are designed to hurt, that harm, that hinder, that debilitate and incapacitate, what is the Church's response?

When young men nonchalantly agress, hurt, vilify and slaughter each other at the slightest provocation, and when young women in particular overtly engage in lewd and lascvicious conduct for material gain, what is the Church's answer?

When Ministers of Religion and Ministers of Government, community leaders and others in lofty positions openly and unapologetically display arrogance, dishonesty and immoral conduct, where is the Church?

As a matter of fact, what is the Church's record in essaying to reduce poverty, mendicancy, despondency and iniquity not just in society at large, but even among its faithful congregationalists / adherents?

And when men demand the right and actually stoop to marry other men, perhaps the greatest abomination, what says the Church?

Yes, why does the Church itself allow, so often and by so many persons, manners of dress and conduct within its very sacred and sacrosanct temples that are decidedly immodest, bordering on the indecent, obscene and disrespectful?

Do these realities speak to the incompetence and irrelevance of the Church in our day and age? Do they attract/deserve anything better than an 'F'?

Perhaps the uncomfortable answer to these concerns lends to an understanding of why there is such a chasmic void in the lives and times of our generation and those abutting it.

I submit that if and when the Church's position is to remain silent at best, or infinitely worse yet, to openly or subtly aid and abet actions that Almighty God Himself clearly frowns upon and expressly forbids, then the Church assumes a position of hypocrisy and irrelevancy, and does indeed earn itself a failing grade.

And this is a recipe for spiritual and moral disaster, a monster that is taking shape, form and proportion on a horrifying scale.

LOVE :- WHICH IS REAL?

Do you love me, or do you not? You told me once, but I forgot.
I do believe that the Lord above Created you for me to love.
He chose you from among the rest Because he knows I love you best.
My love for you will last and last; I'll love you even when time has passed
While on earth, I'll love you so: You'll be loved and beloved wheree'r you go.
A life without you is one of woe, Simply because I love you so.

Yes, as long as ever on earth we live. To you alone all my love I'll give:
And even when we die, I say, My love for you will last for aye,
Yes, when I go to heaven and you are not there, I'll write your sweet name on the golden chair.
And to prove to you that my love is true, I'll come down to hell, just to be with you!

****

Now, is this real love, the kind that God demands?
Or is it, instead, a purely human stand?
If one is willing to die for a human he says he loves,
What about denying life for the Lord above?
For no human being can save our soul;
No human being can make a sin-sick one whole.
And so I say to you, my brethren, here and now,
Let us commit to this very sincere vow:
We'll sure love our family and our fellowmen,
But our love for God will be without end.
Only when we love our Creator truly and sincerely
Can we hope to reign with him eternally!

OUR CULTURE

People everywhere, both present and past,
Cherish and practice some habits that last.
From generation to generation, year in and year out,
These habits and customs constitute our 'culture', no doubt.

Our music, our dress, our architecture, our food:-
These unique expressions truly make us feel good.
Our dance, our dialect our tastes, our values
Are all peculiar features which our culture imbues.

Our people may come, and go our people may,
But our culture, well that is sure here to stay.
It is what defines us, makes us stand out as special;
We must preserve our culture; it's a duty most crucial.

Culture comes in forms that are tangible, sure:
Literature, mannerisms instruments, food, and more.
It's intangible, too to behold, not to be held:-
Our thought patterns, speech forms, lore, heritage.

Our culture bespeaks us it makes us stand out;
It denotes us a people, unique in the crowd.
No nation or society is ever complete, you see,
Without a clear set of features: its cultural identity.

ANATOMY OF A VISIT

On arrival at Aeropuerto Los Americas, which lies some miles outside the capital, Santo Domingo (by which name the entire country is often known and/or referred), I was impressed by its size and layout. An attempt to photocopy the Luis Marin Airport in nearby Puerto Rico, I thought.

And perhaps this thinking was not altogether amiss, for the ensuing 23-day stint in this the first island –country on which the renowned 'discoverer' Cristobal Colon established a settlement, revealed in terms so clear that even the blind could see, that Santo Domingo, which has been declared a natural historic site by UNESCO, gravitates towards and reeks much more of the USA than of the Caribbean, which history, culture and socio-economic realities vehemently suggest that it does.

This anomaly notwithstanding, nothing on Earth could justify or forgive the sweltering mass of the D.R's 7-million-plus inhabitants for their gross and unrepentant ignorance of things Caribbean. Fully 9 out of 10 souls have ears and eyes that never heard of or read about St. Kitts, for example. Bankrupt brains, if you ask me.

And, if I may say so, this 'Republic's denizens wait on ignorance is made pellucidly clear and even more obnoxious by their utter lack of objective knowledge and reality- based information about their very next-door neighbour Haiti, with whom they share a long and, yes, very porous border indeed. Dominicans (not to be confused with the decidedly Caribbean brothers of Roosevelt Skerritt's Dominica!) are satisfied to live with stereotypical images of who / what Haitians, and indeed other Caribbean peoples, are and represent.

Well, is ignorance bliss, or what?
Of course, there are visibly more non - black citizens than Negroid - pigmented ones in the D.R/ (And, admittedly, the golden –brown-skinned lasses by and large are appetizing to the eyes of single men-on-the search, like myself!). Not that this makes any particular statement. But there certainly appears

to be fairly peaceful co-existence between the races of the capital city - even if only perfunctorily.

Superficially, too, there appears to be little crime (as opposed, for example, to the openly violent atmosphere that pervades and saturates Haiti's capital Port-au-Prince, which I had the honoured fortune to visit for 3 days, a welcome temporary respite from the monotony of the course work, which was the raison d'etre for my presence in the D.R). And of course, this creates a feeling of safety, provided one exercises normal, rational care and caution.

Yet, there were few U.S or European tourists dotting, far less thronging the streets of Santo Domingo. Few cruise ships graced the city's sea ports. As expected, I believe, I questioned it. And the answer came, and stayed. It lay in the capital's traffic and utilities-delivery service operations. I gather tourists visit other cities in larger numbers.

Traffic in Santo Domingo is a euphemism for utter bedlam on the road. It is an insane mish - mash of every man to his own order, to hell with everyone else.

There is, purely and simply, no order, discipline or rules on or for the road. No where else in the world, I dare say, even approximates the chaos and mayhem that passes for traffic in Santo Domingo. It is worse than bad. It is unbelievable, pure and total. It does not befit human civilized society.

Pedestrians have absolutely no rights or privileges, not even if it's a school child, an elderly denizen or a handicapped individual using pedestrian crossings. Red light signals are routinely ignored. Gridlock persists at all intentions. Four and five motorists crowd the centre of the road, each going in a different direction, none giving way to any other. Vehicles straddle two lanes at a time, and it is simply common practice to have four and five vehicles driving abreast on a 3 - lane avenue.

Vehicles that are colossal eyesores, which should have been consigned to the trash-heap before Columbus came, cram the city streets. Many have no working headlights, rear lights, brake lights, turn signals, horn wipers, or window - glasses.

They are rusty, dirty, and dangerous. Anywhere else but in Santo Domingo, any way.

I have been a passenger in/ on buses made (but obviously not licensed) to carry 8 persons loaded with 18 passengers, none of whom is a child. And, mind you, this is regular fare, day in, night out.

I submit that this incredible traffic situation keeps tourists out and away.

I myself have, among others, an international driver's license. I have driven in places such as the U.S.A, Canada, Trinidad, Venezuela. But I dare not drive in Santo Domingo. Who, me? Nutten tall go so!!

But there is more that keeps visitors from civilized societies away. Almost every day, either the water supply or the electricity flow is interrupted. Sometimes they combine to put you in real misery by being unavailable at the same time.

The natural though unpalatable concomitant of this unenviable madness is untold damage to electrical appliances. Consequently, very often, hot water baths, televisions, computers, refrigerators, you name it, don't work.

For this reason, almost every single Bank, Supermarket and factory has its own generator. In St. Kitts, for example, generators become necessary only when bad men like Hugo and Georges visit during the hurricane season.

And yet, in spite of these obvious failings, Santo Domingo is worth a visit. Provided one is proficient in the Spanish lingo, he should enjoy a short trip to Dominican Republic.

I find the cuisine a delight. Many tasty, nutritious dishes abound, and at a fair price. A multitude of taxis are readily available to take one to his desired point, while he marvels at the traffic conundrum on the outside. The city itself is rich and replete with history, while it boasts a plethora of shops and stores with a wide variety of items. And the people are generously quite conversant.

So, my stay ended. Maybe you should begin yours, before SANTO Domingo becomes Domingo MALDITO!

The Lesson From Trinidad

For those who insisted that the Caribbean was one Third World region immune to rampant political instability and biting government oppression and ineptitude, and that Grenada was just a unique, isolated aberration in this respect, think again.

The dramatic coup attempt, minority uprising or instance of Moslem intolerance and fanaticism - term it what you will -, the episode of August 1990 corroborates the arguments of many social and political scientists and historians that in any area of the world, especially the Third World, where there is ubiquitous corruption, suppression and non- accountability, there always come a time when the palaces of oppression crumble, when a burning thirst for change and/ or improvement catches fire, and no amount of patchwork or perfunctory performance of duty will extinguish it.

It is still true and beyond dispute that the constant coups and countercoups in other pockets of the Third World, where police states, grinding poverty, brutal repression, endemic civil strife and unbridled corruption and patronage are the order of the day, are, by and large, alien to the Caribbean. But even in this part of the Diaspora, where the masses have a history of passive if not pacific responses to governmental action or inaction, there are groups and individuals, as diverse in strength and size as they are in background and social status, willing to concretize their disgust and vent their frustration at the downpressing system of things by staging attempts such as those in the Spice Isle and the Land of the Humming Bird. As we now see, these courses of action can be violent, bloody and internecine.

And so Trinidad, like Grenada, has lost its innocence. Who's next? Contemporary Caribbean politicians and others who control the levers of power and authority, long accustomed to a pastoral, sometimes paradisiacal political climate and culture, characterized by conservatism and respect for authority, and insulated from the atrocities and upheavals common in Central America, Africa and Asia, for example, must now come to grasps with the reality that they cannot forever ride rough over the will of their citizens and rule the land as though it were their very own; dismissing, if not seeking to stifle, dissent, criticism and opposition. They must understand that many more Abu Bakrs and Maurice Bishops are alive and kicking in their territories, that they have a following, and that they are as convinced of the rightness of their cause as the rulers are about the wrongness of their method to highlight it.

Elections must be free and fair. Efforts to better the lot of the proletariat must be consistent and genuine, and their successes evenly distributed.

No doubt, political awareness of and in many of the islands has now come into sharp focus, especially in countries such as Guyana, the Bahamas, St. Kitts, and Antigua.
It is true that those who would overthrow the system by force sit in jails both in St. Georges and Port-of-Spain. But will this always be the end result? The reverse exists in Cuba, Nigeria, Fiji, and Ghana, to name a few.

I am not espousing armed overthrow of legitimately constituted governments. Certainly not. To take such a stand is diametrically opposed to my Christian conscience. I unequivocally prefer the ballot to the bullet, as the latter tends to mutilate the social fabric and adulterate the body politic. But as we weave the historical antecedents of political behaviour in the Commonwealth Caribbean, we find too many social anomalies that tend to predispose to more Trinidads.

The political directorate has to step down from its lofty pedestal of 'omnipotence' and 'infallibility'! True, the Caribbean's resources are meagre. All the more reason why Governments should exploit them not for the benefit and enriching of a few - as is so often the case - (partisanship, patronage and nepotism are widespread), BUT FOR THE ENJOYMENT OF ALL.

As a student of politics, I see a future where, if the current practices and policies of many a Caribbean government are continued, in more than instances than one, they will be violently stripped of their legitimacy - if any they have - , and the streets of

Caribbean history will be strewn with the litter of Grenadas in 1979 and Trinidads eleven years later.

ISRAEL UNDER SIEGE

These are perilous times for the State of Israel. Of course, ever since its formation, or more correctly its re-establishing in 1948, Israel has not had a moment's rest from a veritable cauldron of abiding hatred and naked aggression hurled at it by its venal neighbours who surround it.

That it continues to exist and survive, and to thrive to boot, is a remarkable story of unprecedented historicity, a miracle indeed, explicable only by the fact that is blessed by the Almighty God Himself (after all, untold numbers of Bible scholars and religious historians agree that the resurrection of the nation of Israel is a direct fulfilment of prophecy, a testimony of the unswerving accuracy of Bible predictions representing the word and will of God), and, until recently, was supported virtually unconditionally by the greatest, most powerful nation on earth: the waning, now sickly U.S.A.

But recent and current events in the geographic locale where Israel finds itself, immovably, (the Middle East), clearly suggest, indicate even, that these are not at all the best of times for the relatively small country.

The upheavals of the Arab Spring of popular revolts, the culmination of years of withering discontent with despotic rule and rotten regnancy of a corrupt political elite, threaten to leave in their wake new sets of rulers and regimes that, unlike their predecessors, are openly and menacingly opposed to the presence and policies of the 'Zionist entity' within their midst.

When one adds to these unpalatable realities, for example, the unrelenting and growing peril and menace of Iran, with its unyielding march and indecent haste towards acquiring nuclear weapons (its vehement protestations to the contrary notwithstanding); the almost-abrupt about-turn of Turkey as a regional ally to a confrontational opponent, and the diminishing strength of the 'special relationship' with and military support of the United States under the current leadership, the outlook for

Israel is bleak indeed.

Moreover, the ever present 'Palestinian Solution' constitutes a perennial, permanent thorn in Israel's very soul, and the Fatah Movement (supported by Israel's implacable foes Hamas) section of the Palestinian Authority's recent essay at the United Nations to make a formal request for that world body to unilaterally approve Palestinian independence, aka a Palestinian State, represents yet another breach being opened in the frontal assault on Israel. Hezbollah, too, has become a formidable opponent.

Together, unequivocally, these form a credible, real and present existential threat to the State of Israel.

But no one in his right mind can objectively believe that such a declaration by the UN will, or can in anyway, contribute far less lead to a solution of the Palestinian issue. Not only will such a move vitiate the standing Declaration of Principles, signed in 1993, which states that the relevant parties would engage only in negotiations to arrive at an agreement on the final status of a Palestinian State. It will NOT put an end to the continuous barrage of rocket and other attacks that Israel regularly suffers from its enemies on many sides. It will not increase the safety or security of Israel or any of its neighbours, and it will not bring the Palestinians one inch closer to their desired   - and legitimate - dream and goal of statehood. The UN vote will not change reality. Chances are, in fact, it will only exacerbate and further entrench the respective intractable positions of protagonists in the matter.

And, of course, any military fallout (conflict or war) as a result of this injudicious step will only serve as a convenient diversion for the tyrants and despots of the region who are being called upon by their own citizens to surrender their vicious, iniquitous grip on illegitimate, oppressive power.

It is expected that our government, alone or in sync with other OECS and/ or CARICOM member-states, will vociferously support the State of Israel in its struggle for fairness, for survival, for peace.

NEEDED - A NEW ORDER FOR 2013

Normally, and perhaps fairly, the New Year ought to signal a new beginning, and should be the reason for hope, optimism, positive expectations, the opportunity to improve on 'old' promising foundations, and to fashion new bases for movement upward, onward and forward.

Especially at this time, coming at is does after the 'relief' that neither did the world end on 21st December (2012) nor did the magnetic poles reverse positions, occasioning colossal, cataclysmic chaos, are thanks and praise in order.
It therefore ought to be that 2013 ushers in a new era of sorts, one wherein lies credible reason and chances for constructive, uplifting pursuits and developments.

Instead, however, we in SKN find ourselves in a most unenviable state of affairs, fed in large part by political chicanery and lending to an atmosphere of distrust, uncertainty and withering discontent on a massive scale.

The problems flowing from this 'art of manipulation and science of government' are, by their very nature and practice, contagious, affecting and afflicting the social, economic and metaphysical dimensions. And for this if no other compelling reason, it is absolutely imperative that country-centred and people-focused solutions and conclusions to this dangerous, untenable position be arrived at the very soonest, and that a new order of things be pursued.

This new system of relationships and interactions must of necessity actively engage the community at large, since their perception of and attitude towards any new reality will be proportionate to their sense of what is true, important, right and wrong. And now, more than ever before, a new political awakening and maturity clearly is taking root and shape, and the immense pressures and crises at this at-times-scary period of transition can only be controlled if the wishes and rights of the populace are taken fully into account.

It appears to me that this new order for 2013 must proceed along the legitimate assumption that we now witness a watershed in political consciousness, a welcome development, but hopefully not too late in coming.

It is my fervent hope and desire that this new awakening in the realm of 'the rule of the majority' and , 'the exercise of power and control' is both accompanied and circumscribed by a set of values which, when juxtaposed, leads to the practice of a love of truth, a sense of justice, a spirit of humility, an acknowledgement of fallibility, a commitment to co- operation, an embrace of personal responsibility, a dedication to serving the common good, and the exercise of accountability.

A new order for the new year sees a nucleus of a great synthesis being wrought, characterized by the combining and converging of synergies and energies that recognize that St. Kitts and Nevis belong to no one man, party or institution, but rather to all of us who truly and dearly love this fertile land that Almighty God has blessed, and cares deeply about.

So that even as the outpouring of a new culture of daring, of alertness, and of passion for rectitude is gaining momentum, we must demand and see it to it that destructive forces of separatism, polarity and narrow partisanship forever take a back seat to unity of purpose and steadfastness of intent to craft a new order for 2013.

Essentially, we need in the new order for 2013 new principles and qualities that can offer to the citizenry safe passage from the crystallized, polarized, internecine forces that have run their course, and a new gateway to openness, security and growth.

May God help us overcome the old and usher in a new order as of now.

NEW YEAR'S WISHES

It is manifestly the case that the Year of Our Lord 2016 does not enter history at the best of times. Beginning, as it does, where 2015 ended, many indeed contend with much legitimacy that this leap year 2016 in fact straddles the worst of times.

Unending and increasing level and instances of unbridled greed; endemic corruption; sexual lewdness; economic constriction; political demagoguery; social selfishness; conceited individualism; religious intolerance and hypocrisy; cultural corruption; family dysfunction, and environmental pollution severally and together paint a dark and dismal but true picture of a humankind awash in a cesspool of moral decay, ethical decadence and spiritual bankruptcy.

Verbal spoutings, comprised largely of hypocritical promises, stale clichés and vacuous platitudes amount at best to empty rhetoric, and at worse serve to create a false sense of hope and security in and among a populace hurting to the core emotionally, physiologically, economically/ financially, and, perhaps unbeknown to most, spiritually. These masses are crying out for relief that is tangible, real and lasting, and are eager to latch on to any utterances or offer of assistance that even smack of the possibility of a let-up in their anguish and their miserable lot. And there is no paucity of such in the mouthings of politicians, religious leaders, philosophers, academicians, military experts and bosses, and would-be pundits of every ilk.

2016 also inherits a reality of oceanic contamination, ecological destruction and natural disasters on a massive, unprecedented scale.

There has been no real change in the ebb and flow of crime, violence, the exploitation of man by man, human and weapons trafficking, drug abuse, domestic familial upheaval, inter-state quarrels, and intra-state strife.

Clearly, neither the Arab Spring, the Occupy Wall Street (and other venues) movement, the machinations of the IMF, World Bank, United Nations and/or it subsidiary organizations, the goodwill of the international voluntary organizations, nor individual interventions have even dented the onslaught of daunting challenges and intractable difficulties that 2015 has bequeathed to its current successor year. One wonders with trepidation whether the new year will witness or produce more of the mountains of bones and rivers of blood that have marred the landscape of human experience again and again.

It seems transparently clear to me that it is definitely beyond the reach and capability of man to 'direct his own step', to solve the problems of the earth; problems, of course, of his own making.

Years, centuries in fact of experiments by and experiences of man in a host of 'isms' and ideologies have proven beyond a shadow of a doubt that, far from creating solutions to problems he is so adept at manufacturing himself, man actually and instead adds to and exacerbates them.

For millions upon millions, life continues essentially to be vacant and lacking in transcendent purpose. Myriads die before they have finished or even really begun to live. For, man's creative genius notwithstanding, it is obviously limited to the material, selective, and transient. Indeed, it would appear that the sages and heroes both of yesteryear and of our day are receding from us, the records of their deeds being contracted into a narrower page. Time and chance, in this evil world, has caught them in a final moment.

The truth is that despite the valiant, genuine efforts of many a man and organization to effect improvement, man's earthly existence is largely characterized and dominated by his inhumanity to his fellowman, his reckless ruining of the earth, and his utter contempt for the message, advice and warnings of the Almighty Creator and His Son Jesus the Christ. There is an abiding barbarism to/in his actions and conduct in almost every sphere of human endeavour, and, indeed, many sport and project their non-reliance on, non-reference to and non-belief in the Creator God as indicative of a superior intellectual sophistication. (A sure recipe for regress now and divine punishment later, if you ask me).

And herein, I contend, is the crux of the matter, which the new year 2016 must face frontally: no effort, no attempt, no intervention by anyone or group of persons will bring real or lasting in/to the lot of earth's suffering denizens unless there is deliberate request for and dependence on the Creator God for His assistance and support.

This means, though, that there is hope. For whereas the past is irrevocably stained with immorality, selfishness, greed, violence, intolerance and destruction, the future is still spotless, waiting and willing to be filled with right and good. And the present, being the place where the product of the past meets the potential of the future, is the occasion to begin.

For the truth, albeit paradoxical, is that behind all the outer chaos and immeasurable tragedy and suffering of 2015 and its predecessor years, now carrying on into the present, the transformative potency of the future, beginning with the present, beckons us to turn to God now, if the rest of the year 2016 and the years beyond it are to be qualitatively different from those up to 2015.

I suggest we so turn with immediacy. This is my wish for all of us in 2016.

THE UNITED NATIONS AT 50

Since the beginning of recorded history some 2500 years ago, man has been at war almost incessantly with the 'enemy' – himself. And this is not just a metaphysical struggle or one individual's volition versus his conscience. Actual armed conflict has been a definitive feature of man's historical experiences from year one.

War is the antithesis of peace. It is the science of destruction and its concomitant, death. Wars, and rumours of wars have been man's lot as the centuries wax and wane. Earlier in mankind's history, it would have been right to confidently avert that only three things in life are certain: death, taxes, and war.

But everlasting war soon awakened the desire for everlasting peace. The stoic Alighieri Dante, Immanuel Kant et al all developed highly-refined plans toward this lofty end. As wars assumed a more global nature, the more pressing became the appetency for an equally global peaceful order.
To this day, the call for one world, unified and at peace, continues fervently and unabated.

It is within this context and a partial response to this call that the United Nations Organization saw the light of day. On October 24th, 1945, six months after its charter was formulated in San Francisco, the United Nations came officially into being upon its ratification by 51 member states.
This week the UN celebrates the 50th year of its debut on the world stage. Has its existence been justified?

It is beyond dispute that the UN is in essence a frail attempt at world government. The perfect achievement of that ideal is admittedly utopian at best, but the United Nations is man's closest approximation thereto. The lesson of history is pellucidly clear and unambiguous: the UN is the quintessence of mankind's human effort at instituting a single unit to run its affairs.

Wars have their raison d' être in causes that are too complex and diverse to be properly and justly explicated, but their diametrically–opposed-alternative, peace, is characterized by tolerance pure and total, and it must be the sine qua non of any hope for a real future.

To the extent, therefore, that the UN has succeeded in preventing a world conflagration of the nature, scope or magnitude of World Wars 1 and 2, it must be applauded. Europe, for example has witnessed , in its history, its first 50 years of uninterrupted 'warlessness', and this fait accompli must be attributed in large part to the influence the UN exerts on its European members as it reminds them of their obligations to its charter.

The world we inhabit today in 1995 is one concerned and obsessed with interests, ambitions, claims, counter-claims, demands, and resistance to all of them. The struggle, in essence, is about power, the love of power, and politics (remember: poli = many; tics=blood-sucking pests!). There is always the need to temper and balance man's id with his ego and superego. And it seemed to some already settled that given the inherent nature of man, which is essentially prone to violence , aggression, and selfishness pure and total , the UN's noble aim of securing world peace was fated to failure ; it was bound to lose.

But as Winston Churchill himself reminds us, survival has become the twin of destruction , and as man came face –to-face with the stark reality that he is 'condemned' to live with his fellowman , irrespective of the latter's ism or ilk, on planet earth, he recognised that the need for this symbiosis must be one of peace. The UN was his idea of the mechanism through which this peace must be procured and ensured.

In time, over its 50 –year tenure as the guardian and guarantor of world peace, the UN has expanded its traditional catalogue of tasks to include, inter alia, peace-keeping operations, elimination of racial injustice, preservation of human rights, supporting refugees, organising referenda and elections, establishing administrative procedures, boosting economic and social development, conflict prevention, preserving and protecting the environment, climate change, and the maintenance and consolidation of peace.

Finally, it must never be lost on us that the United Nations is but the sum whose total goes errant and awry unless its constituent parts - the member states, large and small -   add up, as it were, by abiding by the UN's fundamental principles and policies. The UN and its many specialized agencies can in fact work, but only if its 185 member nations, political and military leaders and the entire world citizenry provide it with the room to manoeuvre, the freedom to act, and the wherewithal to effectively and genuinely be an Alliance for Peace.

"All children deserve and desire teachers who believe that they can learn and who will not be satisfied until they do."

"The TRY-angle will take anyone around the hardest of corners."

(Entry as a student, in an Essay Competition)
THE BANKING INDUSTRY PLAYS AN IMPORTANT ROLE IN THE DEVELOPMENT OF ONE'S COUNTRY

The concept and practice of banking as we know it today has not always been with us, and there was a (long) time in the history of civilization when banking was as alien an idea as that of the airplane at the time of Columbus, for example.

But since the introduction of the innovation called banking in the late 18th and early 19th centuries, it has taken off in leaps and bounds. Banking now exists in every country on earth, and so profound has been its contribution to national development and so crucial is its existence to the economic and social well-being of one's country, that its role in this regard can be considered both phenomenal and indispensable.

The banking industry has been of inestimable value to the growth and development of both developed and developing countries, including those here in the Caribbean, St. Kitts-Nevis being one of them. The industry has been hallmarked by vision, resilience and stability along its journey.

The role of this sector is clearly seen in a number of tangible, concrete ways. For example, the services that banking provides allow and enable persons, families and countries to grow their economy, sustain decent livelihoods, and build their future.

Whether they be Credit Unions, Commercial Banks, Central Banks or others, such well - managed, properly-regulated institutions lend to financial security, stability and success.
This critical role of banks is also seen in the fact that they provide jobs/ income/ revenue for many workers, and job creation certainly is a must for a country's development.

Banks represent the facility that offers a safe, secure place to store people's money, and the mental ease and psychological satisfaction derived from knowing that one's precious monetary resources are safe, enable one to engage in nation-building activities freely and willingly. And more than that, that same money, while being secured, draws interest, which banks provide to savings and other accounts.

Then, by using these deposits/savings to lend to borrowers at higher interest rates, the banks use the profits gained to engage in further lending, thereby providing the means for people to get money to build and/or improve homes, buy land, undertake college or university studies, purchase vehicles, travel, afford medical care, and generally improve their lot. In other words, the banking industry increases a person's life chances.

The industry also often provides sound advice to governments, large or small business houses, and other agencies. This leads to financial security, fiscal prudence, and thrift.

The Central Bank, for example, performs a superlative role in a country's development by being the monetary authority that regulates the nation's money supply, currency flow and strength, and the conduct of its member banks, to ensure financial propriety and accountability. By seeing to the strength of the currency and money supply, frequent – if any - devaluation of currency is avoided. Of course, a stable, viable currency is an important ingredient for development.

The banks are a unique place for savings, deposits and investments. By issuing shares, dividends and interest, by sponsoring numerous community events, by providing scholarships, via social assistance and financial support to governments, NGO's, CVO's, sporting groups, and individuals, banks perform the role of an excellent corporate citizen and partner, and thereby contribute to a country's development.

Moreover, their ATM, debit and credit card, chequing and wire-transfer services, among others, provide ease of financial operations and monetary transactions for wide swathes of the population, and this, too, facilitates development.

The banking sector, therefore, provides financial fuel and impetus for personal and collective development.

This translates into country-wide development, thanks to the role and solid input of the Banking industry.

(Entry as a student in an Essay Competition)
AGRICULTURE IS A VIABLE BOOSTER FOR OECS ECONOMIES

Agriculture, loosely defined, refers to the art and practice of cultivating the soil, farming, producing crops, and raising livestock. It can also include the use of the land, generally, for food production, and has several offshoot dimensions, including horticulture, aquaculture and hydroponics.

Historically, agriculture has played very significant roles in the development and growth of mankind and civilization. Indeed, at certain points in the evolution of man's progress, agriculture was an activity indispensable for survival. Agriculture, its process, practice, product and profitability, determined the construction and institution of man socially, economically, politically, and culturally.

Many societies (including, importantly, the OECS) were for a long time quintessentially agrarian in nature, with the people living off the land, depending on it, caring for it, benefitting from it, living with it.

The truth, after all, is that 'man must live', and his physical and physiological make-up is such is that he must eat to live, and that which he eats comes, can come, from only two sources: the land, and the sea. Of course, even the animals that he consumes, they themselves are dependent on the land for their food and survival.

No doubt it is this simple but profound, inescapable, unchanging and unchangeable reality that led man to harness the potential of the land to provide him with food via a scientific approach, giving rise to agriculture as/in an organized, formal activity.

However, as societies evolved, new developments in medicine, industry and education saw man develop new tastes, desires, values and priorities, tending to a shift away from heavy, intense agricultural practices to more reliance and emphasis on precious metals, mining, oil and gas, et al, for trade and commerce, and profits.

Notwithstanding this general movement away from purely or mainly agricultural activity, of course, man still had to eat to live, and most of his food still came - and comes - from the land. Accordingly, attention to agriculture as the main means of economic returns was never completely abandoned, only lessened. (This, then, provides a ready platform for OECS members to mount in their comeback to agriculture.)

The result, however has been - especially for small states (such as the OECS) lacking mineral resources or industrial might - high food import bills, serious outlay of foreign exchange, loss of cultural affinity to the soil, poor food choices, and an abundance of idle land. These, in turn, result, inter alia, in ills such as high levels of diabetes, obesity, malnutrition, pest (rodent) infestation, overgrowth of idle land, and unemployment.

The OECS, together and separately, represents a miniscule segment of the world both in land area, population size, and economic strength. The nine members of the group collectively number less than 1 million inhabitants, and have a land surface area less than that of any member of the European Union or Latin America, for examples. Their lack of mineral or natural resources and substantial population is significant for its completeness.

But they all possess arable lands in sufficient quantity to significantly contribute to their thrust for economic progress and prosperity.

Moreover, without exception, OECS countries all practised agriculture as a main or major revenue earner for long periods of their history. Indeed, for some, their recorded history is one of agriculture reigning solo and supreme as king, for centuries.

Accordingly, given all the foregoing, it stands to reason that (returning to) agriculture has potent potential to be a viable booster for their economies.

After all, agriculture promises to provide very much of what the sub-grouping needs: job creation; entrenching a historical cultural-economic activity; food security, availability and accessibility; retaining foreign currency; putting lands to good, fruitful use; decreasing health-related problems, and restoring normalcy and profitability to OECS economics.

The OECS leaders must begin now – in schools, colleges, workplaces, media outlets and the general public - to work towards creating in their peoples a deep understanding of, appreciation for, and commitment to returning to extensive agriculture practices as the major means of boosting their fumbling, depressed economies.

Unlike the current activities such as tourism, light manufacturing, financial services and small-scale agriculture, a return to agriculture on a massive, major scale would serve manifold purposes, not the least of which include becoming self-sufficient in food production (thus reducing unsustainably high food import bills) – and remember, we must eat (good) food to live (well) -, and making effective use of our only real resource besides people, our land, by making optimum use of our soil fertility, abundant fruits and herbs and water, and creating much employment, leading to lower levels of crime and the brain drain.

Certainly, this would boost our economies!!

GLOBAL HUMAN INTER-DEPENDENCE

The community, it is said, is the heart of civilized society. But for us, homos sapiens, homo faber, the world at large is the grand stage upon which we all act out this civilization. Some argue - and it is a justifiable argument, given the statistics - that if the inescapable concomitants of 'civilization' are the greed, selfishness, immorality, famine, disease, poverty, violence and oppression which characterize and tear apart man's life today, then they prefer a return to the days of primitive simplicity and deeper fraternity (cognizant of the implications re the absence of many 'modern' conveniences).

But it is to me futile and puerile to debate the merits and demerits of living now in comparison to living 1,000 years ago, for the age in which we now dwell and all its trappings are set and irreversible. And as the debate rages in the halls of academia as to whether 20th-century civilization has justified its existence, what cannot escape the notice of even the most autistic and nescient individual is the magnitude and impact of the evils and miseries that are conspicuous features of our 'modern age', ills that cause the developments in science, medicine and technology to fade in the presence of their extent and minaciousness.

I submit that what is relevant instead to the whole question of man and his civilization is the recognition and an understanding of its very interdependent nature and all that it implies and entails.

The illustrious George L. Beckford postulates in his 'Persistent Poverty', that to have to be dependent on others is dehumanizing. Superficially, this might appear correct. Especially when people like us in this Third World, have experienced the blood-sucking ravages of slavery, colonialism, and now unbridled capitalism, and were (or is it are?) forced to prostrate ourselves and prostitute our culture, sovereignty and identity in return for the aid (not AIDS!) which we are still so very dependent upon.

And, in a narrow sense, Beckford is right. It is indeed dehumanizing and humiliating for anyone to live a life whose very existence, quantity, quality and continuity, rest upon the 'generosity' of others.

Yes, it was and is nauseous and repulsive for the Black of Namibia and South Africa to have to depend upon the vicious, obnoxious racists, who represent an alien minority, for education, jobs, housing ; indeed, their very livelihood.

But upon closer scrutiny, and in a wider sense, we are all dependent in one way to some extent or other, upon others. This applies to individuals, irrespective of size, sex or strength, as well as to nations, regardless of their politico-economic might or geographic area or location. I contend that it is a pure impossibility for anyone or for any single nation to exist totally and exclusively on his / its own.

All life is interrelated, and the message that springs from this interconnectedness is that we all need each other. This is a universally-accepted truism. The United Nations, its aims, objectives and work are but one manifestation of this reality. So that based upon this truth, a question is pertinent: why is there so much selfishness, poverty and war plaguing the world today? Selfishness is a distinctly uncivilized trait. Poverty reminds us so starkly that the rich man wrestles for power and prestige while the poor man scrunts for food in a senseless yet perpetual struggle for the survival of the fittest - and the slickest! Poverty reveals that the distribution of the world's resources is woefully inadequate and unfair, and it thrives because the rich use their wealth and influence to perpetuate a status quo which stinks like stale mackerel on a moonlight night, in its inequality and brutality.

As for war. That course of action is a travesty of the ordinary - and civilized! – civilian's desire for peace, progress and prosperity. It is important that we remember that referenda or plebiscites are NOT a forerunner of a declaration of war, and although the decision to wage it materializes as a consequence of the perverted thoughts and actions of a few, its course and culmination affect all. Humanity is now learning that to wage war on another is to wage war on ourselves. Nuclear Bombs do not threaten the survival of the 'superpowers' only. Oh no! They are minacious to every one on this globe. There is just one world; this one.

People are stronger together than when they are apart. So why be separated? If in unity there is strength, then there must be frailty in fragmentation. The inter-dependence of man, and the need to live it out, must supersede the exploitation of man by man. The practice of selflessness and co-operation must transcend the incessant instances of man's inhumanity to man. The ideal of teamwork is for everyone to perform his specialized role in conjunction with others toward a common cause, a shared objective, a desired end: Universal peace and progress, pure and simple.

Listen to the brilliant Martin Luther King Jr.: "Man's scientific genius has made of this world a neighbourhood, and now, through his moral and ethical commitment, he must make of it a brotherhood."

No doubt we ask ourselves: why hasn't the reality of global human inter-dependence given rise to a greater level of international understanding and co-operation? Why has it not fostered a deeper instance of fraternity among nations as they transact and interchange? Marcus Mosiah Garvey laments that "we profess to live in an era of Christianity, yet our acts are as barbarous as though we never knew Christ."

Kenneth David Kaunda, past President of Zambia, posits that "Society might be able to (some day) conquer poverty and all its offshoots, but without moral and spiritual values, man's life would have no meaning or purpose; the world will not see progress."

I think that the African statesman has forwarded the recipe for the global inter-dependence of man to bear succulent fruit. What is in fact being suggested is that high moral and spiritual values such as mercy, compassion, fairness, understanding, justice, generosity and faith in God must, as a matter of course, guide our lives. No longer must the advice to 'do unto others as we would have them do unto us' be confined to theory. We must transform the high-sounding platitudes into principles that dictate, shape and govern our lifestyle. Anything should be defined not by what it is in itself, but by its relation to other things. For all life is interrelated.

No man is an island. He could be as rich and/or powerful as finite, mortal man can be. No one can truly live according to the maxim: 'I fight alone, I win or sink.' The communist needs the capitalist. The white needs the Black. The Arabs need the Jews. The rich, the poor; the educated, the illiterate. I need you. You need me. The global inter-relatedness of this planet's institutions and inhabitants teaches in an unmistaken way that no nation or people must seek, attempt or even desire to isolate itself/themselves from others. No man must attempt to look down on his fellowmen; only God sits that high.

I am firm in my belief that humanity is not following an unchartered course. Instead, to follow the path set before us, a path circumscribed by time, circumstance and environment, the path of peace, justice and unity, it demands international co-operation and togetherness. We must begin to treat all of mankind's children as citizens of the one world, which we are. Martin Luther King Jr. was right again: "We must all learn to live together as brothers, or we'll die separately as fools."

Let us recognize and act upon the truth that only what is good for all is good for each one.

LET'S TALK FATHERS

There exists in society (ours, at least) a rather vexing and contradictory reality. With one side of the mouth, we wax poetic, pedantic and philosophical about the super-ordinate role that fathers play in the home, and particularly in the lives of our children, especially the boys. We rant and rave about how it is, more singularly responsible than any other factor, the father's absence from the scene, his shirking his responsibility, that results in juvenile waywardness, family dysfunction, and home disequilibrium. We plead and pray in public and in private for fathers to cease being mere sirers of children and to graduate to true, real fatherhood.

Simultaneously, from the other side of the same mouth, we spew invective and hurl abuse at and damn to our hearts' content the said father for the slightest semblance of 'irresponsibility', real or imagined. Worse, we enact and enforce laws that support directly and not-so-directly the criminalizing of the father for the whimsiest and flimsiest of accusations and / or infractions, serving more to drive a wedge between him and his children than as a bridge to span whatever divide his actions or lack thereof may occasion.

Our laws, for example, allow for and even encourage mothers to maliciously, whimsically and capriciously drag fathers before the court for the faintest perceived breach of child maintenance support, with judgment often pronounced against the fathers without lending a sincere or honest ear to his defence/counter-argument, and without due regard to his financial or socio - economic circumstances.

What irks to the core is the practice of the court to order fathers to pay set minimum amounts of money towards the welfare of the child while wholly neglecting to issue a concomitant demand that the mothers fully account for the use of such payments.

It is a widely-known and well-established habit of many a mother to use a father's hard-earned cash not at all for the express purpose of improving the lot of the child, but rather - and so very despicably - in selfish, vainglorious expenses such as doing their nails, styling, etc, their hair, acquiring new clothes and shoes, attending entertainment shows, and other child-neglecting indecencies. Indeed, it is clear that many a mother operates on the notion that the child-support payments are for her to dispense with as she sees fit, without regard to the welfare of the child she claims to love and care for, and acts on the belief that financial support of the child is the responsibility of the father only!

I contend that any survey will reveal that most fathers are adamant that their hesitancy to pay the mothers 'child support' resides in their legitimate concern that the vast majority of the 'support' will in fact NOT be expended on or for the child.

I submit that it is high time that our child custody and maintenance laws be altered to reflect this unsavoury social reality. It is not all solely the father who is to be blamed and condemned as a worthless parent!

We also need to be reminded of the invaluable asset, really, that a father represents in the family scheme of things. Fathers are often reformers in society, embodying the characteristics of being brave, committed, talented, innovative, caring and reliable. A father recognizes that training, supporting and guiding his children is the world's highest calling for a man, and that in teaching, via precept and example, the right and proper principles to his children, he develops in his children the better character.

Real fathers know that the best children, the most successful children, are made by deliberate cultivation. The best children do not grow up pampered by over-doting parents and directed by self. It is the dedicated mind and determined hand of guidance and succour, exercised by the wise father that is the raison d'être of this fait accompli.

Father's heart, just like mother's, loves, rejoices, bleeds and breaks, though often not as visibly. God and nature dictate that the father's role calls for firmness, sternness and courage, but not at the exclusion of compromise, emotion or compassion. The real, true father watches over his children with eyes that never sleep and with a foresight that never slumbers. And, of course, in instilling in his child virtues and values that are indispensable for successful, meaningful living, father himself is schooled by the responses and reactions of the child.

No amount of strong opposition, serious setbacks or staggering blows stymie or stifle the solid commitment of the true, real father to his God- given task. Sons and daughters are made strong and secure by the unswerving dedication of their father to their welfare and well-being.

Of course, father has the advantage of copying from his own Eternal Father, the Father of fathers - Almighty God - in his quest to be a model father, to be a tower of strength and a beacon of light to/ for his children.

On this Fathers' Day 2016, it is ripe and right that fathers be duly recognized for their superlative and supreme contribution to making homes, families, societies and civilization both viable and productive.

Long live the true, real father!

"The problem with being a good sport is that you have to lose to prove it."

THE UNDER-ESTIMATED ROLE OF A MOTHER IN SUSTAINING SOCIAL HARMONY

We here in St. Kitts and the Americas, and no doubt beyond, have just paused to recognize and celebrate Mothers' Day, wherein profuse praise and tributes are heaped ad infinitum on mothers.

Was the attention to, concentration on, fixation and adulation of mothers necessary, justified or meaningful?

That motherhood is indispensable for procreation and survival of the human race is incontestable, pure and simple. But when one examines the true nature, role and responsibilities of a mother, looks deeply at the current state of our social and moral being, and juxtaposes both realities, the candid, objective conclusion reveals that there is more bluster than beef to the chant of "Mother, how great thou art."

For eons, 'home' was synonymous with 'mother'. Home was where mother resided. Where mother dwelt, home was there. Not unwarrantedly, home was to be associated with mother. Given the role and duty of mother, and her being the fulcrum of the home, the latter represented the fortress that shut out the world. It was where the weak, weary, and worn found strength and succour. It was where the plebeian, the commoner, the socially excluded and marginalized, could be a king, queen, equal partner, somebody.

At home, you see, mother 'looketh well to her household' (Proverbs 31:27).

A mother is (supposed to be) endowed with special feminine and solicitous traits unique to the fairer sex and peculiar to the female of the species. These nobly qualify her for the strenuous but honourable task of being the one responsible for creating and maintaining home.

For in as much as the father properly complements the mother, completes the home, and has his specific tasks and functions, both tradition, custom, nature, biology and the Creator Himself are loud, consistent, and unambiguous in their declaration that it is mother who is more largely responsible for nurturing the home.

Some, indeed, contend that the greatest mission of a mission of a woman is motherhood, notwithstanding the simply outstanding contribution that non-mothers have made to civilization and mankind.

None but mother can forge the ties of undying love, unfathomable concern, immeasurable forgiveness, smothering care and inexplicable compromise that weld the bonds of a family.

And, as we all know and agree, the family is at once both the most basic and most important of all social institutions, anywhere. In fact, whereas most other organized entities in society were arranged and established by man, it is God Himself who, in His infinite wisdom, created the family.

Mother is the one, who, via that role, ipso facto, glorifies the Creator and perpetuates His creation (another powerful argument why persons of the same sex should never be allowed to marry). It is mother who makes life possible, then, little by little, alone or otherwise, guides and moulds this new life until it blossoms into noble maturity.

And of course, as she shapes the character of her children, mother also shapes the destiny of nations. It is no idle claim to posit that upon mother and her role does all future progress depend. A mother, by definition and practice, is a woman of industry and grace. This she must be because she must so tenderly and soberly care for her family, especially her children, because they are infinitely precious to her.

Mother is a woman of tact and therapy, for she has many cares to consider, many troubles to soothe and solve, many mazes to negotiate, many hurts to heal. She freely dispenses sensible, lifesaving advice, demonstrates sympathy, inspires, assures, and models right and rectitude.

Mother's lap and/or presence is a masterful combination of nursery, pulpit, classroom, lecture hall, library, study room, discipline centre, and courtroom. Earth's finest school is mother's knee; its most competent teacher, mother herself.

Accordingly, to a very large extent, we are mother made. When mother instils and inputs right habits in the child, they become very hard to break, and, in time, the child is apt to mirror mother. Mother's patient training and positive example, supplemented by sound precept, are indispensable for constructive living and selfless loving as adults, as a people.

It is not difficult therefore, to accept the lament by many - theologians, socials scientists, academicians, psychologists, behavioural experts, politicians, educators, philosophers and criminologists among them -   that the SINGLE LARGEST CAUSE of the abundance of crime, violence, greed, selfishness, immorality, deviance, lewdness and general decadence so rampant in our society today is the absence of the true, real mother, driven by or resulting from a breakdown and dysfunction of the home and family.

For who can deny that far, far more than just a few women who have given birth utterly fail the test of motherhood? Many, many do not muster even 5%.

And this is not just because so very many of them are emotionally, intellectually, psycho-socially, financially and psychologically far too young, irresponsible and immature to even comprehend the role of a mother as herein described. It is also and perhaps more importantly, due to a total disregard for the One who created the family and bestowed on them the ability to be a mother, at least bio-physically.

My position is that schools, the courts, the workplace, and society at large will most assuredly continue to have serious disequilibrium, insecurity, insubordination, indiscipline, indecency and internecine violence as long as the mother continues to be so blatantly ignorant, uninterested, indifferent and/or incapable, with respect to her role as mother, and there is no real support system, programme or facility address this absolutely fundamental flaw and failing of our social reality.

Oh, for more true, real mothers who understand, are ready for and are devoted to their role!

"Never be ashamed of not knowing, but always be ashamed of not wanting to know."

"When you feel too old to do a thing, that's the best time to do it."

"Many a false step is made by standing still."

FREEDOM: WHERE? WHEN?

Former U.S President John F. Kennedy once posited that the single most powerful force in the world is man's eternal, unquenchable desire to be free. And time and again, in both distant ages and in the current era, it is made unerringly clear that man's spirit can be suppressed for years, and years, but that inner, innate yearning for freedom will eventually burst the dam of restraint. And when it does, damned and doomed be those who sought to repress and suppress that desire.

The matter of freedom has profound and far-reaching implications for all aspects of human life. It not only shapes, but determines social, economic and political structures of society, and it dictates the nature of socio-cultural and politico-economic intercourse.

History declares with abundant clarity that the free-er a people, the greater the opportunities for and probability of individual, societal and national growth and development. Even a cursory examination of the rise - and fall - of civilizations, both ancient and modern, leads inexorably to the conclusion that where a people's freedom to choose, to work, to live, to associate, to worship, to move, to travel, to raise a family, etc., is infringed or curtailed, social and economic development is minimized at best.

Why, then, do so many, particularly politicians and the military, so often seek to define and limit the exercise of freedom of their populations?

For even though the level of freedom within a society can never be regarded as fixed or static, but rather should be seen as an evolving dynamic, Cicero's observation that freedom suppressed and again regained bites withy keener fangs than freedom never endangered, holds true forever.

Freedom, of course, does not truly exist where it allows a man to do as he LIKES, but rather to do as he OUGHT. It is the right to BE wrong, not the right to DO wrong. No one has ever been nor indeed can ever fully free to do just as he wishes, since, clearly, that is the recipe for and beginning of chaos and anarchy.

Here in St. Kitts (and Nevis), we generally tend to view ourselves as being free. But, really, free in what sense? To what extent? Isn't it the reality that we are free only in so far as to do what the laws of the land permit?

Freedom in practice is linked to the capacity for the individual to more fully express his indwelling spirit.

In some societies, man is not free to even think, without consequence. His very thoughts and thought patterns are circumcised by tradition, laws and beliefs. He in indoctrinated to think and act along certain prescribed lines.

Significantly, throughout the ages, man has fought even to the death for the right to be free, for both himself, his contemporaries, and generations yet unborn. To date, no one anywhere at any time has been born in chains!

The Arab Spring of the last few years reveals that the desire of many to be released from those suffocating, unnatural strictures on the exercise and expression of free will is strong enough to bring even long-entrenched dictators, tyrants and freedom-suppressors and repressors to their knees.

It has well been said that for freedom to be fully and properly enjoyed by any person, it must be available to everyone. And of course, as (Abraham) Lincoln reminds us, he who denies freedom to others deserves it not for himself.

The old adage that eternal vigilance is the price of freedom has also stood the test of time. Certainly, here in St. Kitts and Nevis, we enjoy a number of freedoms. That is, we can express freedom in a number of ways that are still denied millions in other countries, some economically worse off and others yet better off than we are.

The truth is that notwithstanding the fact that much of the misery, poverty, pain and suffering being experienced by sizeable portions of humanity is imposed and maintained by a deliberate curtailing of freedom, there is ever the hope and the expectation that sooner or later, then there will come a time when the palaces of oppression and suppression will crumble, when liberty catches fire, and freedom will no longer be for many, a thing far more ardently to be desired than seriously to be expected. After all, there is a growing belief that the main purpose of politics is really not the maintenance of law and order, or even the facilitation of economic progress, but more so to guarantee freedom to/of/ for the populace.

Let us cherish, protect and preserve the freedoms we now enjoy, and dedicate not to deprive others (save criminals, of course) of relishing theirs.

"Only two times to praise God: WHEN YOU FEEL LIKE DOING IT, AND WHEN YOU DO NOT FEEL LIKE DOING IT."

"Force without justice is tyranny; justice without force is impotent."

GANGS IN RETREAT?

The Gang (Prohibition and Prevention) Bill 2011, currently before the National Parliament and open for public scrutiny and comment, aims to deal a telling blow to the vicious spiral of criminal violence engulfing the nation and fraying the social fabric by making it illegal - a crime itself - to be a part (leader, member or follower) of a gang, to encourage others to become a part of a gang, or to discourage others from ceasing to be a part of a gang - by whatever means.

The Bill is fairly comprehensive in scope, punitive in nature, prescriptive and proscriptive in tone, and, I dare say, noble in intent.

Of course, some may argue, with merit, that the Bill comes as too little, too late. But certainly it represents a robust piece of legislation, which, rigidly, impartially and consistently enforced, should result in a marked decline in overt gang activity and operation in the not-too-distant future.

The truth is that, clearly, not all instances of crime, violence, drugs and/or gun use are gang- related. In fact, these ills and evils have been our coevals for decades, preceding the arrival and growth of the gang phenomenon by many years. But the reality also is that the introduction and proliferation of gangs have brought to their territory and left in their wake concomitant exponential rises in the incidence of violence against the person, notably involving deadly gun use.

In the absence of hard, empirical evidence to the contrary, it is safe, based on obvious trends, developments, circumstances, scenarios and other factors and variables, to not just assume but conclude that it is the insane, idiotic, senseless gang-on-gang rivalry that has spawned the unprecedented levels of shootings, wounding and homicides fast threatening to become the order of the day, such that give our Federation one of the very highest murder rates per capita on the Blue Planet.

The Bill, in its wisdom, not only penalizes membership, etc., of/in gangs, and seeks to prohibit and prevent their survival, but also, importantly, attempt to offer alternatives to gangs/gang activity, thereby encouraging real or potential gang members to divert to more wholesome, socially-acceptable, personally-redeeming courses of action and behaviour.

After all, there can be no elimination (of gangs and the 'belongingness' they provide) without substitution, and in this connection, adequate resources - expertise, training, funding, etc. - must, consciously and deliberately, be made available to encourage the formation/ strengthening of family kinships and to secure the maintenance and flourishing of community organizations with relevant, meaningful programmes and projects that attract, benefit and retain present and/or would- be gang members.

The point must be laboured again and again that NOT being a part of a gang has infinitely more good and the capacity for good both now and in the future for ALL, including gang members themselves as well as the rest of society, than its dangerous alternative of gang membership.

Specific to the Bill, however, I wish to strongly recommend to its framers and those who will eventually enact it that the section that makes it an offence to be a member of a gang when that person is a law-enforcement officer, be complete by adding "or a TEACHER in any formal institution of learning."

I also suggest that the Bill, with specificity, allow for the expulsion from any such institution (of learning) any student who is found to be a member of a gang. (Depending on his/her age, the student may be re-admitted upon evidence of having ended gang membership).

In addition, the manifest role of parents it in the fight against gangs must be emphasized. So that, for example, where a parent is found to be indifferent to his child/ children's being a part of a gang, or where he (the parent) does NOT actively discourage such gang membership (of his child/children), he (the parent) is obliged, in the first instance, to attend counselling/instruction classes or courses. Of course, more severe penalties accompany persistent delinquency in this regard.

In any event, it is well recognized and is now settled opinion that the current state of affairs in our dear land is utterly untenable, in so far as gang activity is concerned: young men, nonchalantly snuffing out the lives of other young men; young men resident in certain areas cannot freely or safely move to other areas of their community or of this (very small!!) island without fear of execution; wholly innocent residents are slain as collateral damage in this mad gang warfare; familial ties, social bonds and social intercourse are severely interrupted as many persons stay at home for fear of being caught in the crossfire - in the 'wrong place' at the 'wrong time'.

There is no doubt that the Bill at issue, or its enforcement, is no panacea for the crime and violence that afflict the land. But it sure constitutes a promising tine in the multi-pronged effort aimed at reducing same.

May it find safe passage and non-discriminating application.

"The best way to cheer yourself up
is to cheer up other people."

WHITHER, CARICOM?

More than just a few grave issues of formidable consequence and import currently - and for some time now - challenge the Caribbean Community.

CARICOM has been with us in excess of forty years, but that its record boasts more shame and failure than achievement and success (particularly when juxtaposed against its essential raison d'être) is a posit that needs neither defence nor explanation.

CARICOM, for all intents and purposes, seems to have gone. Long time.

Because, really, the simple, poignant, direct question is: In what concrete, tangible, palpable way has CARICOM benefited the average citizen, the 'ordinary' man of the region?

Certainly, CARICOM can readily present a plethora of agreements, declarations, resolutions, and the like, that flow from its myriad meetings here, there, and everywhere. But for eons, there is a nauseating paucity of translating lofty, and, for the most part, noble enunciations and proclamations into real, visible or meaningful action.

For example, the Charter of Civil Society, adopted in 1997, remains a document yet to see the light of day with respect to honouring via observance, its 23 articles.

The so-called CARICOM Passport is a colossal joke. So-called citizens of CARICOM are meted out no less uncivil, brusque and disdainful treatment than others of far flung territories when visiting other CARICOM member-states. Save for the exemption of the requirement of a visa for visiting, those of us living in one CARICOM country, when visiting another 'sister' country, are subject to the same - and indeed, in many instances, infinitely worse - excessive and often dehumanizing reception at points of entry as are persons hailing from the furthermost recesses of the Blue Planet.

The incessant, obnoxious behaviour of many immigration and customs officials towards CARICOM visitors is nothing short of selective discrimination and harassment, pure and total, on a massive scale. The recent highlighted incidents involving Guyanese, Jamaicans and others visiting Barbados, Antigua and others are but samples of this phenomenon that makes a complete, filthy mockery of CARICOM-ism.

In theory - and only there -, CARICOM regards strong, robust and flexible institutional capacity as sine qua non for good governance and CARICOM workability, but the unfailing tendency of governments and leaders to cling tenaciously to a moribund philosophy of 'sovereignty' and territorialism (to the point of being intoxicated therewith), renders the probability of this theory being converted to active reality far more ardently to be desired than seriously to be expected.

The current state of the West Indies (CARICOM) cricket team and the CCJ re the exercise of its appellate jurisdiction, for example, are potently symbolic of the de facto state of affairs of CARICOM, especially as it relates to being of definitive worth and benefit to the typical CARICOM citizen.

Truly, how can anyone convincingly refute the argument that CARICOM, as currently constituted and operated, is in an advanced state of fragmentation, riven and driven by centrifugal forces carried by economic implosion, petty, narrow nationalism, and political cowardice? Concentric circles function to create a false sense of community, aided and abetted by the conspicuous absence of the salutary influence of visionary, selfless political leadership.

It is unpalatable, but accurate to declare without compunction that, generally, those of us who have the fortune – or misfortune - of inhabiting these CARICOM isles and other land masses feel no real connection to, experience no real advantage from, and see no real meaning in CARICOM.

Neither the young nor the not-so-young, student, businessman, profession, amateur, affluent or indigent, common or elite, can point with any conviction to any fount of comfort that is derived from or dependent on CARICOM.

As we traverse the various domains of the realm, we cannot be blamed for sensing the crying need for oneness, for unity, perhaps for a 'king' to reign and rule.

Sadly, no such 'salvation' beckons from the horizon any time soon.

We shall perhaps have to await the rise of new, enlightened generation with the requisite political will to experience the real potential and benefits of CARICOM.

Unfortunately, by that time, no doubt, CariCOME would have certainly been CariGONE.

"To acquire the habit of reading is to construct a refuge from almost all the miseries of life."

A 'BLACK HISTORY 'MONTH'?

'Black History Month' has just passed. Or has it? For herein lies the problem: it is patently insufficient, farcical even, to select one month per year and attempt to 'celebrate' 'Black History' therein. (In any case, why don't we in this part of the diaspora designate our own period(s) to emphasize our own Black History, from our perspective?)

'Black History Month' purports to highlight, commemorate and celebrate the inputs and outputs of Black people into the melting pot, the cornucopia of human achievements.

And certainly, this is a necessary and noble ideal. Because for centuries, the superlative contribution of blacks to the development of civilization and the enriching of the human experience has been deliberately under-reported, conveniently de -emphasized.

But the fact of the matter is that no one, no race, no ethnic group has been beaten up and beaten down, lied to and lied on, messed with and messed up, abused, misused, refused and confused, anywhere close to the reality of the Black experience. This experience is one that encompasses the contradictions and pain of 'discovery,' conquest, racism and state brutality, and the travails inherent in the dirty institutions of slavery, colonialism, apartheid and neo / quasi-apartheid.

Not only is there no doubt that the scourge of the enslavement of Africans (indisputably the ancestors of most of us) for unpaid labour is an unsightly scar on the history of mankind and a permanent blight on the seared consciences of the colonial perpetrators. In addition, just as inarguably, the victims of the worst forms and expressions of the exploitation of man by man and of man's inhumanity to man have not only survived indescribable atrocities visited upon them, but have risen to heights celestial and achieved feats unmatched by his erstwhile oppressors and downpressors.

And so we need to commemorate and celebrate the experiences. This is our right, our duty. But just one 'month' per year? Can one month suffice?

These commemorations and celebrations are essential. They remind us of human misery, yes, and that the heart of man is desperately wicked above all things. But they also are a part of the ongoing healing process, and represent a step in nation-building. Permanent closure to the experiences we and our forebears underwent may not be possible, but ensuring that we never forget them certainly constitutes an instrument for the healing of wounds and embracing of all earth's denizens as worthy of respect and dignity.

What has been the response of Black people to these vile and vicious attacks on our personhood, dismantling of our way of life, deprivation of our freedom, and reducing of our humanity to chattel?

This valiant unparalleled attempt at recovery assumed multiple forms. Negro spirituals, the Black Power Movement, Negritude, Civil Rights, Peasantry and Unionism are but some of the developments that served to restore pride and strength to Black people, providing avenues and vehicles to transport them/us back to the heights of prominence where we historically, rightly and justly belong. These, inter alia, served to offer an ecstatic celebration of the sensory, social and spiritual values inherent in blackness and black culture.

For example, the individual and collective contribution of Blacks to and their achievements in the following areas are unprecedented and incontestable: Sports, Medicine, Education, Literature, Music, Theatre, Science, the Military, Politics, and Business and Industry, among others.

Our colossal creative inventiveness is seen – and felt - daily in numerous products and objects. These include – but are in no way limited to -   the ironing board, lawn mower, type writer, peanut butter, paints, lotions, soaps, pencil sharpeners, pressure cookers, fire extinguishers, locks, the elevator, shoe lasting machine, gas mask, traffic signals, guitar, bicycle frame, air conditioning unit, internal combustion engine, bottle caps, refrigerator, mop, telephone transmitter, and hair brush. These are but a sample of the long list of indispensable items created and invented by Blacks.

In every age and every land, men who are Black, of Negro or African descent, have thoroughly distinguished themselves. For example, where would the world be without luminaries such as Pushkin, Dumas, Aesop, Nefertiti, Amenhotep, Mansa Musa, Shaka Zulu, Toussaint L' Ouverture, Menelik, Banneker, McCoy, Frederick Douglas, Dubois, Owens, Tubman, King, Garvey, Parks, Poitier, Woods, Bradshaw, Simmonds, Bolt, Collins, and literally countless others?

Of course, one 'month' cannot do justice to the exigent commemoration and celebration of these Black brothers and sisters, past and present.

Admittedly, this is not to give the idea that all is well within the Black community at home and abroad. Certainly not, for it is painfully clear for all to see that more often than not, Blacks have pursued policies and practices that have resulted in mountains of bones and rivers of blood. Today, untold numbers of Blacks suffer immensely at the hands of other Blacks.

At home and abroad, the Black family, the Black man and Black youth in particular engage in behaviours that not only hurt each other, but decidedly insult, retard, demean, diminish and stain Blackness and the Black cause.

For this reason, Blacks have not realized their full potential, and do not experience the kind of peace, progress and prosperity that beckon, if only we learn from our ancestors' experiences, exploits, advice and warnings!

It is, indeed, wise to recognize that those who do not learn from history are bound to repeat it.

As Blacks, we must stop abusing our talents, our bodies, our brothers and sisters, our opportunities, mother earth and her resources, and the mercies and loving-kindness of our Creator God.

In our needed, duty-bound attempts to commemorate and celebrate our experiences and achievements, and to carve four ourselves, our children and generations yet unborn a future bright and blissful, we must consciously lay aside the issue that divide us, conscientiously build on those that unite us, and confidently forge our way upward, forward and onward. And we need more than a 'month' to do that.

"If courtesy is truly contagious, we should start an epidemic."

"We need higher wages to pay the higher prices occasioned by higher wages."

"An angry person is seldom reasonable; a reasonable person is seldom angry."

"ASSESS THE ROLE OF JAMAICANS IN THE CARIBBEAN EXPERIENCE OF THE PAST 50 YEARS"

It is, in my estimation, beyond dispute that no account of the Caribbean's historical experience, be it of the near or distant past, or of current times, is even contemplatable far less complete without reference to Jamaica and its unique and singular contribution to what is collectively the Caribbean experience.

This input by/from Jamaica in actuality spans the gamut of the Caribbean's history from 'discovery', settlement and colonialism, to post-emancipation, decolonization, pre-independence, and post-independence. But specifically to the past fifty (50) years of Jamaica's attainment of political independence, that Jamaica and its people have had a significant say in crafting and shaping the Caribbean is a fait accompli, and warrants no defence.

In August 1962 (subsequent to the collapse of the West Indies Federation), Jamaica preceded Trinidad & Tobago in severing the colonial bonds that subjected (or is it subjugated?) it to the 'Mother Country', Great Britain, by becoming a free and independent member country of the world community, assuring leadership of its own internal and external affairs, and being master of its own destiny and captain of its own fate. Its first Prime Minister was the Hon. William Alexander Bustamante.

In so doing, Jamaica led the way for the English-speaking countries to follow in exercising the rights, privileges and responsibilities of full sovereignty. Jamaica blazed the trail in this respect, for indeed, among all the islands of the Caribbean, only the two countries that occupy Hispaniola (Haiti in 1804 and the Dominican Republic in 1844) had achieved that feat before it.

And, of course, since then, all members of CARICOM, save Montserrat, beginning with Trinidad and Tobago, have followed that route.

Over the past 50 years, Jamaica has led the region in several other areas as well, in very conspicuous ways, in the process of solidifying their role in the Caribbean experience.

For example, Jamaica was at the table of the 1st Conference of Heads of Government of CARICOM not long after its establishing in 1973-1974, along with Barbados, Guyana and Trinidad and Tobago. Its leader then, Michael Norman Manley, became a well-known vociferous champion of Third World and Caribbean agenda, ensuring that the region was represented at important world fora such as the United Nations, the Commonwealth, the OAS, and the ACS.

Jamaica was also a part of the group of four Caribbean nations which defied threats and western policy by affording diplomatic recognition of Cuba in the mind 1970's.

Jamaica also spoke for much of the Caribbean in its unrelenting opposition to the inhuman system of Apartheid practised in South Africa for several decades, right up to 1990.

The University College of the West Indies, precursor to the magnificent University of the West Indies, was set up in 1968, with Jamaica (at Mona) naturally being the site of the largest of the three Campuses. (The others being Barbados and Trinidad & Tobago).

Jamaica, with its immediately-recognizable black, green and gold flag, has seen an impressive number of its nationals, both at home and in the Diaspora, boast a litany of achievements by individuals and collections of individuals which, collectively, speak clearly of a colossal contribution to things Caribbean.

These inputs easily override and supersede whatever non-constructive developments certain characters would have occasioned. For example, the negative 'vibes' emitted by the likes of Christopher 'Dudus' Coke, Vybz Cartel, and Ben Johnson, inter alia, are readily overwhelmed and transcended by the enviable feats of the likes of Usain Bolt, Percival James Patterson, Jimmy Cliff, Portia Simpson, Louise Bennet, Roderick Rainford, Kenneth Hall and Rex Nettleford, among many others.

These latter-named individuals are but a sample of the repertoire of talent and expertise that Jamaicans have inputted in the Caribbean experience over the past half-century. Some of the most excellent performances and productions in the fields of sports, politics, entertainment, music, literature, academia, dance, cuisine, culture and economics have been contributed by Jamaicans.

Where would the Caribbean – and the world - be without reggae, ska, track and-field sprinters of extreme velocity, and ackee? These all originate or at least are strongly associated with Jamaica!

It is no surprise that Jamaica was the first Caribbean island to field a team at World Cup (soccer) finals.

It is also quite understandable that the late and lamented Emperor of Ethiopia, his Excellency Ras Tafari Makonnen Haile Selassie I opted to plant his feet on the soil of Jamaica in the said year 1962 when he first visited the Caribbean. After all, not only was Jamaica the largest and most powerful of the region's territories politically, economically and culturally, but, and no doubt more importantly, it was the land where the Rastafarian movement had its Caribbean genesis, and from whence the faith's influence and roots spread to every single other island and country in the region over the years. (Of course, the followers of Rastafarianism regard Selassie as their Supreme Divine Being.)

Jamaica also played a critical role in the invasion and occupation of Grenada in late 1983, in collusion with the OECS territories and the Untied States, in the aftermath of the self-destruction of the Grenadian Revolution, culminating in the assassination of the then Prime Minister, Maurice Rupert Bishop. Jamaica was then, as it is still arguably now, the lead military power of the region.

Further, the distinct, unique accent and vocabulary of the Jamaican tongue is not only instantly recognizable but also actually a welcome ingredient in the Caribbean melting-pot.

Many contend that the Caribbean is not the Caribbean, certainly not complete, without Jamaica. Many persons in far-away - and not so far away! - lands know only of Jamaica as an island country of the region. They are blissfully ignorant of the names or identities of almost all the others! Many citizens/nationals of other Caribbean territories are obliged to cite Jamaica as a point of reference in describing their geographic location.

Accordingly, it can be seen that Jamaica's contribution to the Caribbean experience is powerful, singular, and lasting. It is beyond dispute that Jamaica represents a hard act to follow with respect to its influence and input in the development of the Caribbean over the past fifty years.

Congratulations to Jamaica and its people on the attainment of their Jubilee of Independence.

"Imagine! : these (current times) are the good old days we'll be longing for a few years from now!"

THE WHY's of a MONUMENT

French Historian Jean Michel Dereau aptly describes the transatlantic Slave Trade and the Slavery it sustained as "the greatest human tragedy in human history." He is supported in that view by the lamented historian of Caribbean renown, C.L.R James, who argues that slavery was a "dirty institution".

In St. Kitts, the population is, inarguably, of slave descent. The vast majority of the populace are sons and scions of African's denizens, and are as essential an element of the Diaspora as any.

Given these realities, and as the year 2007 signals the 200th anniversary of the Abolition of the Slave Trade in the British West Indies, of which St. Kitts was the 'Mother Colony', that a monument to the epic struggles of our slaves ancestors to emancipate themselves from forced bondage is apt and appropriate, needs neither defence nor explanation.

This monument, to be erected in the central locus of the buying and selling our forefathers as animate chattel -   Pall Mall (now Independence) - Square,) in the city centre, will represent the unending stoic resistance to the vile system of slavery, and its eventual vanquishing.

The objectives of the constructing and presence of this monument in this historical space include, but are not limited to facilitating the following:

To serve as a permanent link between our historical past as an enslaved people and the development and achievements of the now.

To bring to the physical fore a greater conscious awareness of Kittitians of their history, and its place and importance in the history of the civilization of mankind.

To cement a deeper understanding and appreciation of their national identity and heritage.

To present to visitors and locals alike an additional cultural, aesthetic and meaningful attraction of historic worth to Basseterre.

To provide a sense of closure to the process of healing of the nation of the scars etched in our collective psyche re the experience of slavery.

The locating of the monument in the Square will also function to appease the spirits of our progenitors, who restlessly agitate for resolution; to cause the current citizenry to revisit and contemplate the factors that led and still lead to enslavement, with a view to eradicating it from the earth; and to instil in generations yet unborn the need - nay, the duty - to be ever conscious of and grateful for the efforts and contribution of their predecessors towards creating for them the conditions to enjoy a safe, secure, and progressive future.

Build me a monument!

"No one is born bad, or ever becomes bad all at once."

"Failure: The chance to do better next time"

"Every man falls at some point. The mark of a real man is that he gets up each time and keeps going!"

Is There Hope for Africa?

An amorphous aggregate of humans, largely confined – not condemned! - to the negroid race, straddles a continent that is relatively young, a continent of immense potential wealth but actual, inexplicable poverty; a continent struggling for survival.

Africa, dubbed the 'Dark Continent', is the second-largest of the six that inhabit the earth, and its massive land mass more than quadruples that of near-by Europe, whose kings, emperors and presidents carved up - and then not too neatly ! - the area and allotted to themselves and to each other parcels of huge chunks of real estate.

Some argue that it is this historical division by Europe, and the subsequent colonialism, slavery, capitalism and cultural imperialism that served as 'Certificates of Permanent Doom' to Africa, and left in its wake a socio-economic and politico-cultural structure that predisposes to endemic poverty, backwardness, disease, economic instability, political inelasticity, coups and counter-coups.

Certainly, Africa cannot contend that its state of impecuniosity derives from a lack of human or mineral resources. That claim may be posited by other pockets of Third World under-develop-ment, notably the Commonwealth Caribbean.

And, unlike Communist societies, for example, whose poverty can be traced to an inefficient economic structure, Africa's state of want is more attributable to the lack of an economic infrastructure that supports a wealth-producing process.

Yes, by and large, Africa, particularly sub-Saharan African, wallows in misery and destitution, while its erstwhile masters, having raped and plundered African societies of much of their riches and resources, frolic in the water of superfluous abundance.

Africa does not seek exaggerated luxury, nor even unbridled success. For the time being – and that is all millions of African citizens can contend themselves with, as the future looks too distant, too bleak, sometimes absent -, this too- neglected continent would be satisfied if it could only feed its rising multitudes, house them, educate them and sanitise their surroundings even to the barest minimum of comfort.

Instead, the 'Black Continent' is riddled with diseases, not the least of which is the dreaded AIDS. Its flora and fauna are threatened and endangered. Witness the merciless slaughter of elephants in particular, and the rapid decline in acreage of woods and forests, as a deprived and dispossessed section of the Diaspora cut down and burn trees for fuel and timber.

There are indeed countless reasons to despair for Africa, from which so many seek to flee, but often fail to even make the attempt in the sure knowledge of the reception, or lack of such, awaiting them in their would-be 'havens of rest' , were they fortunate enough to survive the trip in the first place.

At the beginning of the current decade, per capita income in the 45 countries south of the Sahara Desert is less than $300 (U.S). Although its production of food fluctuates according to the dictates of weather, market forces and political stability
(Africa is still largely a peasant society), it is still the world's least successful producer of the commodity.

Gains made in health and education in the immediate post-independence era have been lost to economic anaemia, cultural hemorrhage, and a dizzying population growth rate. While the Sahara creeps south, the Kalahari crawls to the north, portending even more horrendous living conditions in the years ahead. Africa en bloc is more dependent on foreign assistance than is any other part of the developing world.

Of course, there have been many Africans who have made their mark on the world scene, men whose contributions have left footprints in the sands of time. Gamal Abd El Nasser, Kwame Nkrumah, Nelson Mandela, Jomo Kenyatta, Julius Nyerere and Wole Soyinka count among the continent's illustrious few (that is, in recent history).

But, truth be told, Africa has also given birth to some of the world's most brutal, mercurial and racist of men. Idiot Amin, Jean-Bedel Bokassa, Muammar Ghaddifi, Hendrik Verwoerd, Balthazar John Vorster and Macias NGuema come to mind. These men were the direct cause of the atrocities that have given rise to Africa's mountains of bones and rivers of blood.

It would seem to many, no doubt, that a dearth of highly-trained and very adept technicians, technologists, intellectuals and scholars lends itself to the sorry state of affairs that is the panorama of the African socio-political landscape. For years, many have rallied to the cry of 'educate the masses' as though its implementation constitutes the panacea for all that ails, as though it entails the recipe for success pure and total.
(I am yet to be convinced that a high or even full literacy rate is a concomitant, prerequisite or consequence of lack of want. Witness Cuba, Canada, U.S.A, for example.) (This, of course is not to be so naive or dishonest as to dismiss the worth and necessity of education).

Be that as it may, the reality, pure and simple, is that the crying needs of the stomach for nutrition, and of the body for refuge from the elements, are more pronounced and urgent than the nourishing of the mind, and thus take precedence over them.
What, then, is Africa's hope? Or did that too escape Pandora's Box with respect to Africa? Can this land mass of over 800 million souls continue to depend on the 'benevolence' of richer nations? After all, we are reminded by George L. Beckford in 'Persistent Poverty' that to have to be dependent on others is dehumanising!

Why can't the oil of Nigeria, diamonds and gold of South Africa, for example, be exploited and maximised for the optimum benefit of the Lost Continent? Don't tell me that it is not that simple, for making things difficult for one another is not only a glaring instance of man's inhumanity to man, it is one of the processes that pain the body politic and make life miserable and hopeless for untold myriads.

It has long been apodictic to reiterate that Blacks and Africans are in no way a sub-species of God's creation. We are inferior to no one. Far from it. In fact, in many ways we are a sturdier people than some. But sheer force of circumstances, many too complex to unravel, converged to create a status quo where, among all peoples of the Blue Planet, Africans are the poorest lot

Can the situation be altered? Or is this an irreversible course of events?

If we learn anything at all from history, the answers are a thunderous YES and NO, respectively. For the Soviet Union, for example, is more than 70 years old, and it still reels from serious problems of all sorts. The mighty U.S.A, another example, is heading for its third century, yet huge economic and social anomalies exist, to the extent that they threaten to diminish its superpower status in the long, maybe short run.

Africa, after all, is still young, barely a generation in existence. And although the world economic structure – designed and controlled by the rich few – does not favour the poor, I have abiding confidence in Africa's ability to extricate itself from its morass and improve its lot. That it will eventually do so I rest assured, for no condition is permanent.

(Penned in 1988)

500 YEARS LATER (1992) (Consequences of Columbus' Error)

The most Elementary student in the Americas in general and here in the Caribbean specifically, has heard of Christopher Columbus in some form and at some time or other. The name is much more known and recognized than those of many of our local or regional stalwarts, the latter's relatively recent appearance on the stage of socio-political activity notwithstanding.

Many of these students, probably the most senior ones, are also aware that Columbus' arrival here 500 years ago was not the outcome of a planned or deliberate objective, but rather the momentous consequence of a massive blunder, of a mistake that turned inestimably sweet for the European powers in whose name the new 'Indies' were claimed. In fact, Columbus was attempting to convince a sceptical world of a fallacy, part of which involved the magnificent folly of his 'Empresa de las Indias', and part of which revolved around his tenacious belief that the route to India from Europe was shorter due west than east.

His error was the rediscovery of America, and it signaled the beginning of a new era in world history, with colossal, immeasurable consequences for mankind. Indeed, Columbus' 1492 feat was a remarkable historical event that ushered in the Modern Era, in a very real sense.

And this is what makes Columbus and his epic voyages significant and commemorable. For notwithstanding the episodes and periods of the most glaring example of man's inhumanity to man, which, too, were a concomitant of the process of discovery, colonization and settlement (wherein the discovered ones were the victims), the Genoese sailor's four trips down south made the vast Spanish Empire possible and opened up a new age and a new page in the history of the world. It furthered the conquest of western civilization, which explains why the racial ethnic cultural makeup of this aggregate of the diaspora (the Caribbean and the Americas) is the way it is. It also elucidates the reason and factors that predisposed the region to its current state of economic backwardness, political inelasticity by and large, and a cultural inferiority complex.

Yes, this first contact between the 'old' and the 'new' worlds so altered the course and content of history as to forge a crucible of ethnic diversity for all the major races of the world. And in as much as this led to unspeakable suffering for the colonised masses then and thereafter, it also forced mankind to look into its soul and construct within its midst new multiracial societies with entirely new social contracts that are now, hopefully, better equipped to lead us into the 21st century.

(Out of this multi-ethnic eclecticism, for example, was born the greatest and most pluralistic society ever - the United States of America. Today, the developing societies as well, including the Caribbean and Latin America region, can lay claim to a joint heritage, and a mutual prospect that is strengthened and enhanced by the richness that arises from a mixture of cultures and races which essentially and eventually emerged from the voyages of the man called Columbus.)

Moreover, according to Adam Smith (The Wealth of Nations), the 'discovery' of America and the Cape Route to India are "the two greatest and most important events recorded in the history of mankind". This importance resides largely in the clash of forces it released, and the new, seemingly inexhaustible market for European goods it furnished, leading in turn to that effect which was "to raise the mercantile system to a degree of splendour and glory it could never have otherwise attained."

All this, it must be reiterated, is not to dismiss or even de-emphasize the miserably negative effects that Columbus' coming had on the lives and lifestyles of the original inhabitants of the Americas: the Kalinagos, Caribs, Arawaks, Lucayans, Mayans, Incas, Aztecs, and Indians .

But the fact also is, (and this, too, must be taught to the rising multitudes of the schools' populations), that the rediscovery of the Americas, 500 years old this year, ranks
without competition as the greatest event of the millennium.

A WORLD ADRIFT! WHAT TO DO?

How many of us here in St. Kitts, elsewhere in the diaspora or throughout the world take the time to engage in moments of reflection, meditation, and introspection? What percentage of us reserve for ourselves a period to profoundly interest ourselves in the manifold happenings and trends around us, near and far?
Is it that these events and developments are too esoteric and abstruse in nature, they seem too far detached, or we are simply too busy or disinterested?

Because when we examine what is happening in and to nations great and small, to peoples everywhere, to our land, seas, air, homes, school, workplaces, arenas of entertainment, churches, attitudes, tastes and values, we cannot but wonder why, what is the meaning behind all of it, and what it forbodes for generations to come, for the future of humanity.

The secular humanists among us consider man to be the measure of all things. (Of course, measured against any yardstick past or present, man, when weighed in the balances, is found very wanting!)

But the truth is that despite the mind-boggling wealth of a few, the seeming success of others, the apparent comfort of some, and the clear selfish apathetic indifference of many, significant numbers of the Earth's denizens have grown more sceptical, uncertain, pessimistic, and fatalistic. They are steeped in doubt that human reason, ability or effort can provide any integrated, meaningful worldview of/for existence, or of/for the ills and evils that characterize it. It is transparently clear for all to see that man cannot properly or successfully govern himself or rule the earth that sustains him. Many a man deliberately continues to wilfully hurt and harm his fellow man. The world is awash with men who are professors, but not possessors, of virtue.

They play on honesty and when they are dishonest. They purport to champion our causes, but in fact they trample them.

Many a man's expenditure of rhetoric seriously exceeds his income of ideas, and many quote scripture but neither believe nor practise it.

So although the universe is undoubtedly endowed with purposeful life and consciousness, it would appear that mankind in general has missed the essence and corrupted the uses of both. The menagerie of forces that constitute this phenomenal world that God gave us seems unable to get across the lesson that man IS his brother's keeper, and that man must care for, not abuse Mother Earth.

I suggest that unless, with alacrity, we shift focus and change directions, the growing levels of distrust, greed, immorality, pollution, violence, selfishness, mismanagement, and intolerance - among many other evils - will eventually overwhelm, suffocate, and destroy us.

We need, immediately if not sooner, our moral and spiritual bankruptcy (the real reasons for/causes of our problems) to be replaced by individuals, groups and organizations dedicated to the proposition that a new age of enlightened thinking must dawn, leading to actions that result in the physical, social, psychological, economic and spiritual upliftment of humanity, hallmarked by palpable progress towards synthesis, cooperation and compassion for all life.

To neutralize the jeopardy that confronts humanity on its relentless journey to atrophy and self-destruction, we must start now, individually and collectively, to visualize and work tirelessly towards creating a world of inclusion, commiseration, and consideration for/ of all others.

Admittedly, it is a tall, perhaps even difficult calling, but it is one to which we must respond with haste and sobriety if we are to bequeath to our children and our children's children a world that is sane, safe, secure and stable.

Leaving No Child Behind, Regardless!

I am as delighted as I am humbled by being bestowed with the singular honour to be the guest speaker at this very important and highly significant occasion organized by the men and women of Operation Future, the latest in a string of useful and progressive innovations of the Royal St. Kitts and Nevis Police Force.

I would wish to begin, or rather proceed with this brief address by extending and expressing profound congratulations to these whose vision and passion facilitated and qualified the creation of Operation Future.

As I understand it, this concept has as and at its core an abiding and fundamental interest in and concern for the welfare of our children, the nation's most precious resource.

Here, the aspirations and actions of the Police Force merge and mesh with mine, and I dare add, with those of the Ministry of Education, with whom and for whom I have worked all my life.

As has been intimated by the Hon. Minister himself in his earlier presentation, the well-being of our children occupies the continual attention and exacts significant expenditure in cash and kind of the political directorate in general, and more specifically and more directly, of the Ministry of Education.

Ladies and gentlemen, I am firmly of the view, and I declare it here and now, that children are God's gift to society as a cogent and concrete indication that he wishes that there be a future.

I am an unrepentant and incorrigible supporter of Sophocles when he affirms and asserts that "Life's aspiration come in the guise of children". Mahatma Ghandi himself it was who advises: "If we want to have real peace in the world, we shall have to begin with the children."

And so, in my mind, any action that targets children, students, especially primary school children, if that action is positive, constructive and progressive, if that action is void or devoid of ulterior motives and/or malicious content on intent, any such action is worthy and worthwhile.

I put it to you today that Operation Future is one such action, and, ipso facto, it is to be embraced and supported.

Like the Drug Abuse and Resistance Education project before it, Operation Future aims to instil in students, particularly primary school students, the critical point that there are adults who care for them and care about them, who want them to succeed, to do well, to grow and mature into decent, law-abiding, justice-loving, compassion-possessed citizens, and who would brook no opposition nor spare any effort to ensure that they our children are provided with the safety, security, support and solace requisite for that growth and success.

The sad fact is, however, that too many adults either do not understand, appreciate or welcome their role in this scenario.

Too many parents, far too many mothers, fathers and guardians, have relinquished their God-given and society-mandated role to nurture and nourish our children socially, intellectually, and spiritually in a manner that conduces to mental, physical and emotional strength and stability.

The fact of the matter is that again and again, too many parents attempt to absolve themselves of their sacred, immutable responsibility by abandoning their duty and neglecting their charge.

I call upon parents to cease and desist from the unacceptable complaint and cry that "I can't go with him"; "she too much for me".

The simple question is: If you as a parent, with the legal and spiritual authority to "go with him", decide that you can't, who can? More importantly, who should?

I contend, if in fact I submit that you CAN go with him. But it must begin at birth, in infancy.

Operation Future, however, in its wisdom, recognizes the inevitability of some parents and guardians falsely believing and acting upon the belief that "they can't go with him/her", and so it has come on stream to contribute meaningfully and tangibly to the fight to ensure that no child is left behind.

It is dangerous at the very least for St. Kitts as a country to be moving ahead and moving on economically and otherwise while leaving even one child behind. That one child, left unattended, may eventually be the source of untold suffering for /of millions.

Yes, it may be only normal and natural for one or more to fall by the wayside, but such an outcome must never be the outcome or result of negligent or deliberate action. And even then, he must not be bypassed as a matter of course.

Instead, sober, serious and sensible organisations such as the Ministry of Education and the Police Force, entities such as Operation Future are committed to the principle that, as Martin Luther King Jr. so eloquently put it in 1964, "I cannot be what I ought to be until you are what you ought to be."

The national motto of Antigua and Barbuda sums up this philosophy in the words, "Each endeavouring, All achieving."
To you the students, I want you to know that we your parents, teachers, police officers, Sunday and Sabbath School instructors, we adults, we care for you. Even when we seem to be rough, tough, stern and strict at times, we love you. We believe that children like yourselves have to be constantly supervised and corrected, and that punishment is absolutely necessary as a component of that correction. We have learned that under everyone's outer hard shell is someone who wants to be loved and appreciated.

We I, want you to learn that love, not time, heals all wounds. I want you to know, to learn that the easiest and best for you to grow as a person is to surround yourself with people who are smart, sensible and decent.

Learn that life is tough, but that you are tougher. Learn not to let opportunities pass you by. Someone will surely take the ones you miss! Learn that for you to reap well tomorrow, you have to sow good deeds today. Learn that the only place where success comes before work is in the dictionary. Learn to love God and serve Him, learn to love yourself. Learn to support Operation Future. Thank you.

15th Sir Arthur Lewis Memorial Lecture and Awards Ceremony
(Welcome remarks at ECCB)

It is, truly, a singular and special delight for me to be here this evening, to share the stage and this historic moment on this auspicious occasion.

An illustrious audience of such prominent and distinguished guests, invitees and participants such as you who constitute this august congregation certainly makes the evening and the event superlatively significant.

Of course, having in your midst, in our presence, a personality of the reputation and calibre of Dr. Michael Clemens, as this year's lecturer, only serves to add circumstance and quality to this unique moment of note.

Ladies and gentlemen, Governor and staff of the venerable ECCB, Dr. Clemens, I am therefore particularly pleased and definitely delighted to bid a supremely warm welcome to all of you here gathered for this much-looked-forward to occasion of the 15th Sir Arthur Lewis Memorial Lecture and Award Ceremony.

It is no idle boast, mere cliché on trite platitude to announce and pronounce our Federation as two of the most delectable and desirable destinations and paradisiacal islands on the Blue Planet. St. Kitts and Nevis have proven time and again, that we list among the top most friendly, hospitable, savoury and captivating of peoples and countries of the universe.

This is so not only because of the innate predisposition of our people to be affable and reliable, not only because of excellent leadership in our various spheres of activity, not only because we are bent on keeping our environment clean and civil, but also due to the contribution made by visitors, residents and tourists alike, all of whose efforts combine to render our two small islands veritable oases in an otherwise desert of confusing conundrums.
And so I welcome one and all and particularly our guest speaker to St. Kitts and Nevis and to this exercise.

Of course, we in the Caribbean, wherever the diaspora is settled, are immensely and eternally proud of the legacy of Sir Arthur Lewis, the St. Lucian/ Caribbean patriot stalwart who stood tall and strode confidently on the stage of world affairs and ideas, especially as they relate to things economic, the essence of his contribution being so profound, so meaningful and so universal as to earn him the Nobel Prize in Economics.

In obtaining what is arguably the world's most prestigious prize, Sir Arthur proved definitively that the Caribbean has grown from being a relatively mere bucolic academic outpost, to a region with intellectual talent that rivals and equals that anywhere else on Earth, including the most advanced and affluent countries.

The ECCB, then, representing as it does the critical mass of the region's denizens, is actively contributing to providing the knowledge and analysis of the dynamics of economic trends, developments and movements by organizing this forum on a regular basis.

I am sure that all of us look forward to not only hearing from Dr. Clemens, but also eagerly anticipate learning from the various interventions that accompany the 21st Annual Conference of Commercial Banks in the region.

Mr. Chairman, it is true that if we look only at the surface of things, we derive at best a superficial view and cursory understanding of the nature of things, and it is inevitable that we feel a deep sense of inadequacy in the face of the stupendous challenges that we face, especially in these times of economic depression, recession, and, may I add, suppression.

Indeed, it is with a keen sense of optimism that this year's lecture and conference sessions will provide us here at the ECCB, in St. Kitts and Nevis, and throughout our beloved Caribbean region, with credible, practical suggestions and recommendations as to the way forward, that I reiterate my work welcome to all.

May you have a tremendous successful series of activities, and may the blessings of Almighty God attend our every effort. Thank you.

In Remembrance of Labour's Fallen Stalwarts

Brothers and sisters here congregated this lovely afternoon in the historic village of St. Pauls, I greet you pleasantly and cordially in the name of our Lord Jesus Christ, whose benevolence, ineffable love and limitless mercy are responsible for our still being on the land of the living, still inhaling the breath of life.

And I propose that this idyllic community named for the Apostle Paul is historic if only because it has given to our proud Federation two of its better leaders, one of its two Prime Ministers, and its first National Hero.

I must therefore pause to congratulate and thank this quaint village, St. Paul's, for having contributed in no small measure to the development and progress of this country by providing us with leaders possessed of the vision and wisdom to spearhead that development and effectuate that progress

We have come here today, as duty demands and conscience obliges, to commemorate the lives of and pay tribute to our fallen heroes, our late and lamented leaders, mentors, and brothers, namely: the Rt. Hon. Robert Llewellyn Bradshaw; Hon. Caleb Azariah Paul Southwell; Hon. Joseph Nathaniel France; Hon. Clarence Fitzroy Bryant; Hon. Lee Llewellyn Moore; and the Hon. Edmond St. John Payne.

But let me hasten to add and to assure you that notwithstanding our focus, if you wish, on these past outstanding leaders, we do remember, as we must, the sterling contribution to nationalism, national development and nation building by other politicians and party stalwarts whose individual and collective efforts combined to ensure that the Federation of St. Kitts and Nevis assume pride of place as it sits astride the platform of upward, onward and forward movement.

Let it be recorded here and now that Labour, on behalf of the masses of the country, registers its eternal gratitude for the unique and superlative contribution these deceased patriots and compatriots have given. May those of us beneficiaries and inheritors of the legacy of our interred predecessors commit and determine to continue the struggle for the financial, political, intellectual, economic, spiritual and mental emancipation of our people.

I wish to remind all of us that these former giants on the local and regional political stage operated at a time when it was really not opportune to do so. It was no bed of roses for Bradshaw, Southwell, France, Bryant and the others to devote themselves to political action in order to realise economic liberty for the ordinary man.

Let the youth, our children and students of today understand in unambiguous terms that the freedoms and opportunities they enjoy today did not come easy. Let them understand that their life chances in 2006 exist because of the sacrifices of our fallen heroes back in 1956, 1966 and 1976.

Bradshaw, Bryant and the others did not enjoy the luxuries of perks, privileges, pomp and personal gain that many contemporary politicians pursue and possess.

They came up against a colonial authority not disposed to their modus operandi. The global economic and political order was not at all favourable toward their aims and efforts. Yet they persevered. And they succeeded.

Let this be a lesson for those of us who occupy positions of power and authority today.

The party must forever be vigilant in ensuring that it remains what its architects and founders envisaged and devised it to be: an organ of representation, an institution of support, a vehicle for upward mobility.

We must forever keep our focus on the needs of the people whom we lead and serve. We must subsume self and selfish interest for the greater cause of the common good.

And we, like Bryant, Bradshaw, France, Payne, et al, we must persevere and abide.

Ladies and gentlemen, the great, indomitable Shakespeare once lamented that 'the evil that men do lives after them, the good is interred with their bones.' (Julius Caesar).

Well, Southwell was, as we all know, an avid student of Shakespeare, to the extent that he quoted his writings frequently, and actually named his children for several of his characters, finally naming one of his very own sons Shakespeare, for the bard himself.

However, Southwell delighted in pointing out where, when and how Shakespeare was wrong in his enunciations and sayings.

And I submit to you today that Shakespeare was again wrong when he used the words quoted above.

Because I wish this afternoon to laud and applaud in particular the contribution of the late Hon. Clarence Fitzroy Bryant, lawyer, educator, sportsman, bridge player, Minister of Education, Health, Social and Community Affairs, Attorney General, political stalwart, child and product and symbol of Labour.

Let me not labour the point but simple remind you that by emphasising the contribution of Bryant to Labour, to public service, to nation development, to nation building, does not, because it cannot, diminish in any way the contribution of any or all of the other stalwarts.

But, you see, this year 2006, we celebrate a remarkable achievement in the field of education, an outstanding feat accomplished in the education area, one whose genesis finds its roots in the mind of Bryant and whose growth is attributable to his unending effort to ensure its fruition.

We celebrate this year the 40th anniversary of the introduction of Universal Secondary Education (USE) in the Federation.

This was, and is, a development that was as phenomenal as it was revolutionary.

In 1966, St. Kitts and Nevis had not yet even entered into associated statehood with Anguilla. That was to be the following year. At the time, we were still firmly planted as a colony of the mother country, Britain, with little internal autonomy.

But Bryant, being the visionary educator and concerning, caring politician that he was, oversaw the introduction of USE at the Sandy Point High School, thus heralding onto our social-political landscape a truly novel and welcome component - Universal Secondary Education.

This USE, of course, essentially ensures that all, not just some, not 50%, not 75%, not even 90%, but that all students leaving or completing primary school have free access to secondary school, that all students graduating from the primary level of education are assured of a place in high school, that secondary education is available to all our students, in irrespective of class, colour or creed.

You see, before Bryant brought USE on the scene to St. Kitts and Nevis, only a selected few, the elite, we say, could access post-primary education. Poor, ordinary people, like Bradshaw was, like Douglas was, like I was, like most people from St. Pauls and most people of St. Kitts were, could not go to High school, no matter how bright we or you or they were. There was simply no room for every Jack and Jill who wanted, who deserved to go to a secondary school.

But Bryant, Clarence Fitzroy Bryant, bucked the tide, as it were. He defied the odds. He faced the challenge. He introduced USE, thus making it possible that all our boys and girls, your sons and daughters could go to High School when they leave our primary schools.

I want you to imagine for a moment what it would be like in St. Kitts if today in 2006 we still had a situation in which only 10, 20 or even 50% of our boys and girls had to 'stop from school' as we say in local parlance, when they were finished grade 6. No high school, no secondary school, no Cayon High, no Sandy Point High school for them.

I am sure that you agree that that would not be a pretty picture. In fact, that would be a nightmare. Well, we have the like Hon. Clarence Fitzroy Bryant to thank for that. But I'll tell you more, brothers and sisters. St. Kitts and Nevis is nigh the smallest member country of the United Nations and the OAS, and one of the smallest in the Commonwealth,

CARICOM and even the OECS. Yet, we are just one of very few countries, just four I am advised, in the region with Universal Secondary Education.

Antigua only recently introduced it. St. Lucia in fact sent a high-powered delegation here earlier this year to learn from us just how we have managed it so well, because they are thinking of introducing it there – in phases – starting September. St. Vincent still has some way to go to boast of USE. Other countries are years away.

And the list goes on. Our small twin-island state is a pioneer in this matter, as it is in so many other areas.

And so in , 2006, we celebrate 40 years of USE, and the Ministry of Education, which I have the honour to serve at this exciting time in our history, deems this a momentous occasion, one worthy of commemoration.

In fact, a committee of able persons, chained by educator Michael Blake, is in place, organising relevant activities to celebrate the occasion.

I am advised that the activities include an Education Conference in October, a television documentary in November, and the launch of a commemorative magazine in December. Also, between September and December this year, there will be a series of debates among secondary school students, and panel discussions, involving others.

Brothers and sisters, USE is no small thing. It is no wonder most of us may take this reality for granted, because it has been with us for so long.

But I want you to understand that USE means that we can present in a structured, formal way to our young people, especially during their teenage years, information and knowledge of a nature that helps them to pursue meaningful careers, take up special jobs, and contribute to our society, economy and country, skills, talents, competencies, abilities and efforts that we need to survive and thrive, but which simply could not be taught or implanted at the primary level.

So that, in essence, without Universal Secondary Education, we simply could not have the quality or quantity of workers that we boast today.

It is appropriate, therefore, perhaps even incumbent upon us the beneficiaries of USE to express our innermost gratitude and appreciation to comrade Bryant for his foresight and prudence in placing and presenting USE on our educational plate.

40 years is a long time. Many people these days do not live to celebrate their 40th year.

We therefore owe a deep debt of gratitude to all our predecessor Labour heroes for their exemplary demonstration of good governance in all aspects of government. But this year, today, I wished to turn and focus the spot light on the late Clarence Fitzroy Bryant.

We stand today at the pinnacle of Caribbean Educational Achievement, and we owe this accomplishment in no small measure to the colossal spirit of commitment to education excellence of this man.

It stood to reason, of course, that the College of Further Education – where students enter, having passed through secondary education - be named for and in his honour. And that institution itself, the Clarence Fitzroy Bryant College, today shines as a beacon of light, the epitome of academic sophistication, in the sub-region.

Yes, we cannot ever over-state the contribution of Bradshaw, Southwell, France, Moore, Payne, Bryant and the rest to the development and building of our dearly beloved country.
Today, as before, we say "thanks a lot" to them. We must commit to keeping their spirit and legacy alive. Certainly, we look forward to another 40 years of USE, building on what Comrade Bryant started.

I commend the lives and works of these stalwarts to us all. I commend their spirit to the God from whom it came. May their souls rest in peace.

An Education for Peace

The International Year of Peace is here. It comes at a time in the history of the Blue Planet when peace, pure and total, universal, abiding peace, is a thing far more ardently to be wished for desired than seriously to be expected. For 1986 was born in era of cacophonous warmongering and peace –shattering behaviour by nations and individuals, unprecedented in modern times.

For too long, eloquent speeches pleading for peace have given way to the superior might of action and preparation for war. Amidst this hypocritical and dangerous state of affairs, voices are being raised in protest and are asserting themselves. These voices may not be loud, but their clarity and sincerity are unmistakable. Their message is unequivocal, unambiguous and undeniable: Mankind desiderates peace.

Not the peace that is found in stones, trees and other inanimate objects. That is a dead, intangible peace. Not the fragile, temporary peace that is defined as the absence of war. Oh no! We seek the peace that is vibrant and dynamic, the supreme peace, the peace that passeth all understanding.

I am of the opinion that to achieve or acquire this type of peace should be our objective, and that we should use formal and non-formal education as instruments in pursuance thereof. We must unite humanity by teaching children about peace and human rights, whilst at the same time respecting the principle of plurality of ideas.

In 1986, war rages ubiquitously. Human rights are flouted in the four corners of the globe. Millions of refugees eke out an existence in so called host countries. Millions more are cruelly subjected to conditions which rival slavery in their levels of degradation, distress and indecency. The stinking system of apartheid still thrives, and billions of dollars are expended on machines of misery and murder while myriads suffer from ignorance, poverty, homelessness, hunger and debilitating diseases.

Amidst this recondite system of things, a call is made for sense and rationality to supersede the madness. People find this call magnanimous and applaud it, but no one wants to commit himself.

But when fighting for an idea – an idea as abstract as peace, even - , one must be courageous, consistent, and effective. The battle for peace is not waged with guns and bombs, but by the strangulation of greed, selfishness and vanity, and the emergence of a sense of and commitment to justice, co-operation and humility.

Human beings are not born racist, violent or arrogant. They adopt these behaviours during socialization, and so our education system must be designed to inculcate the virtues of fraternity, tolerance and the oneness and inter-connectedness of man. Our education process must emphasize to its participants and recipients the fact that they share equal citizenship of one and the same world, and that they must express solidarity with the victims of oppressive and repressive state systems and political demagogues.

Our education must be an education for creativity, originality and independence, but it must also be an education for peace. It must enable the society-at-large to acquire a knowledge of the international significance of human rights, and give children a sense of responsibility and a feeling of worth.

Our mental faculties must be clear of all notions of bigotry and of any complex. We must be fair and sober, rational and considerate, for peace rules the day where reason rules the mind.

Oldest Student Returns Top Grade (1999)

The humble village of Saddlers sure has reason to rejoice these days. One of its senior citizens, almost-60-year-old Iva Stevens, affectionate and popular in the community, was among the hundreds of residents writing the Cambridge G.C.E O-level exam in English this past June.

Iva, who was tutored by educator Michael S. Blake, excelled in the exam, and was one of the small minority who received the highest score – Grade A - on her exam.

In doing so, she put to shame scores of other students, many of whom could be her grandchildren, by surpassing their respective grades. Her performance also vitiates the notion by many senior adults that they are 'too old to learn'.

Her tutor, Mr. Blake, whose students in English had a pass rate of 85.7%, one of his higher rates of success in the annual exams, say he never for a moment doubted her competence and her ability to pass the subject. She was ready to listen, easy to teach, quickly to learn; an attentive and industrious student.

Iva might just be the oldest student to have written the G.C.E O-level exams, and obtained the highest grade possible – at least in these parts; certainly in her native village.

The Prime Minister, in whose constituency she, Iva, resides, beamed with satisfaction and pride upon learning the good news.

It is expected that Iva will be rewarded in some tangible way in the immediate future for her outstanding accomplishment. It is hoped that her performance will serve to encourage older persons to sign up for special lessons and emulate her feat.

Iva's family, friends, her tutor Mr. Blake, the Prime Minister and this newspaper commend and congratulate Iva on her unique performance.

(Reprinted from the Labour Spokesman newspaper, September1999)

Quality vs. Quantity in Educational Outputs

Schools are the only social institution expressly concerned with providing to its student clients, in a structured, formal, systematic way, a package of information, knowledge, attitudes and experiences of the relevance and quality requisite for meaningful, tangible contribution to the development of the individual client himself, the community he inhabits, and the national good.

Of course, a perfunctory look at examination results, aided and abetted by carefully presented statistics, might lead those satisfied with the cursory only, to conclude that schools in fact, by and large, do discharge their prescribed role.

Nothing could be further from the truth.

The contention here is that education's mission is essentially a four-fold one (the academic / intellectual; the vocational preparation; the inter-personal/co-operative; and the personal/moral development), and that in neither of these dimensions can it boast of excellence in its output.

In far too many instances, the spotlight is on the **quantum** of outcomes rather than the quality of performance. Yet it must be emphasized and reminded that even in the domain of quantity, the results are far from satisfactory, since the fact of the matter is that the number of students writing and passing exams, or indeed even completing secondary schooling, is often much – and frighteningly - removed from the numbers that started off the formal learning process 10, 11 or 12 years earlier.

And it must long be abundantly clear to all concerned that the difference between those clients who started (at age 5 or thereabout) and those who finished (at age 17 or so) more often than not manifests itself in/as a feral underclass of non-achieves whose conduct and behaviour, born of a lack of social skills, technical know-how, academic prowess, or marketability, represents a sub-cultural underbelly of the body politic. But the immediate concern, really, resides in the reality that even among those who get to the point of writing and passing exams, the quality of the results is decidedly mediocre at best. Few, in few subject areas, record excellence of quality. (Certainly, for five or ten students to pass all subjects taken with the highest grade possible cannot be construed or accepted as success of/in the education arena, not even in jest.)

It seems to me that what is lacking is an unambiguous, unwavering demand for, commitment to, and expectation of excellence at all points of the education continuum – from student discipline, student attitude, student performance, student achievement, teacher quality and devotion, principal leadership, parental involvement and societal support, to uniformity, consistency, validity, and impartiality in assessment and grading - in order for quality to characterize outputs, to be at its highest possible, and to transcend quantity as the benchmark for success.

All instructional leaders and practitioners must be fully and unequivocally dedicated to the proposition that every child/student can learn, must be appropriately taught, and must be maximally assisted and facilitated to achieve his fullest potential. This approach must take deep root at the very earliest stages of the teaching–learning enterprise, and must govern any strategy for/of delivery of information, creating spaces and opportunities for learning, etc.

A dashboard of critical performance indicators that triggers immediate corrective intervention must be developed and executed alongside a regime of robust inspection and appraisal of the teaching process and institutions of learning as a matter of urgent priority in the thrust for quality over quantity.

The truth is that far too many students, especially males, are not being adequately serviced by the educational apparatus, leading to plenteousness of male marginalization and under-achievement. And of those who go through to fourth or fifth form, exam passes notwithstanding, too many are leaving functionally illiterate, maladjusted, lacking in social graces, unprepared for the world of work , adulthood and parenthood, unexposed to and unready for the challenges and vicissitudes of a modern economy, complex society and ever-changing, technologically-sophisticated world.

All this, I submit, because of a misplaced emphasis on and acceptance of quantity of outcomes more so than quality.

"No one has ever been deemed 'great' except he has rendered service to the human race."

"He who does things that count usually does not stop to count them."

Education and Male Marginalization -- A Connection?

It is manifestly the case that all is not well with our education system, especially in so far as it relates to its utility, value and effect on a large number of our males.

The contention is that the high and growing number of our young men liming the block, occupying the street corners, engaging in violence, committing crimes, filling (and overfilling!) the prisons, populating gangs and otherwise presenting/displaying plenteousness of wastage-of-potential and an abundance of idleness are, arguably, the outcome and output of the system in mal-practice.

Is there merit to the claim by some that the education system assumes a 'learn, or leave' posture, with in-built features that encourage males in particular to opt for the latter offer? Is the complaint true that males must either cram, or scram? True, many important, worthwhile lessons valid for success in life cannot be and are not taught in schools; but then, why are they not caught, either, especially by our males?

And why is it that in spite of a plethora of retreats, discussions, symposia, conferences, and other fora, replete with an excess of reports, declarations and resolutions, quality teaching and learning seem unable to graduate from theory to practice?

Does the answer reside in the fact that education decisions - many of which serve to shape if not determine the academic, social and economic future of education's clientele - are often not research-based or evidence-grounded, but driven by whims, fancies, beliefs and emotions? Certainly, there are several approaches that need to be adopted, some with expeditious immediacy, others with urgent haste, in order to arrest the marginalization of our males as an outflow of our education thrust.

For example, the quality of teachers must be enhanced. At the recruitment stage and thereafter, focused, deliberate training and appraisal must be the order of the day. Teachers must be taught and obliged to stop expecting and forcing students to learn according to/depending on how teachers teach, and start teaching the way students learn, including having cognizance of and paying attention to the principle of multiple intelligences. They must possess and exercise the will and the skill to adopt this paradigm shift.

Super-emphasis must be paid as a matter-of-course and a matter of fact to how and what pre-schoolers and kindergarteners learn, as the student's capacity to glean and assimilate information, his earning potential, outlook and behaviour as a parent, adult and worker are laid - or flayed - at these formative stages of development.

It is also at this critical juncture that special attention must be directed to the male student. He, in particular, must no longer be made to 'sit still' and 'keep quiet' in the very false belief and hope that that very unnatural, 'unboyish' and unchildlike posture facilitates learning. The truth is that it stymies and frustrates it, the effects rising to the fore in the teenage years and beyond in a massive but undesirable display of aggression, ignorance and intractability.

Both the process and structure of education must be forensically re-examined, for clearly, the returns on our colossal collective national investment in education are neither satisfactory nor tenable.

It is my unwavering conviction that we must candidly and objectively interrogate our purpose, content, delivery and evaluation of education, and I am confident that in the process, we will have to conclude that our males are too easily and too often left on the verge.

Single-sex schools for boys, as a remedial, palliative counter-measure, for example, must be fashioned out of the chaos that now obtains.

The fact that all of our young men who enter into gangs, drugs, guns, crime, violence and murder with reckless abandon are products of our education system, itself represents a clarion call and crying need for us to stop, introspect, reflect on and genuflect to the obvious imperative to cease creating and perpetuating a system that, deliberately, incidentally or otherwise, facilitates the marginalization of the male of the species.

Indeed, "Jack and Jill went off to school, to learn and be taught together,
But that did not turn out so cool, and Jill soon bested her brother.
Jack's peculiar styles and needs weren't met, but Jill's the teaching seemed to prefer,
With the result being that Jack, you bet, in under-achievement did slide deeper.
In academics and behaviour as well, the girl regularly outshone the male child;
And the norm has been, as the records do tell, the latter has sure lagged far behind.
So now, seems clear, to save the male, we must return to single-sex instruction.
'Twill serve, no doubt, as years of yore regale, to save the male from marginalization!"

"The world will be an infinitely better place were the power of love to replace the love of power."

Violence in Schools: -- Assessing the Problem

Schools, of course, are expected to be safe havens for students and teachers, a home away from home, in both literal and figurative terms.

For many students, the home environment is toxic, bitter, and detrimental to their general well-being, and schools are not just the only institution where structure, order and discipline are to be found, but they also are expected to be in large measure nests of security and comfort that conduce to learning and where the flux of human nature manifests itself in interesting, challenging but meaningful and constructive ways.

Schools are also expected to be moral centres, reinforcers of positive values, paragons of virtue, and models of discipline where teachers, operating 'in loco parentis', care and nurture.

But if the truth be told, in many of our schools -   perhaps in all, to some degree -   a number of forces and factors converge and combine to create an environment which approximates that expected of a den of iniquity, a palpable characteristic of a cesspool of incompetence.

The reality is that more than just occasionally, students and teachers alike are both victims and perpetrators of violence that is verbal, emotional, psychological, intellectual, and/or physical, at times entering the realm of the criminal.

And, since children live what they learn, there is little doubt that those who regularly experience violence will practise it in their everyday interaction, sooner or later.

It is the latter type of violence (i.e. physical, bodily violence), of course, that historically attracts the most attention, concern and umbrage, as it appears to straddle the matter of life and death far more so than any other form of violence.

In some schools, there is a stifling feeling of insecurity and fear that often leads to teachers and other students refusing to intervene in and speaking out about clear, open, known cases of violence of multiple sorts. (This attitude and approach, naturally, works to perpetuate, even exacerbate the problem, much as obtains in the wider society - of which schools are microcosm - wherein a mortal fear for one's safety has created a culture of silence even when one directly witnesses a criminal act.)

In several schools, there are not-so-small-numbers of students who neither study nor work. They breach school rules, major and minor, with reckless abandon. These students almost always eventually prove to be ones suffering from exclusion and marginalization, feeling no affinity for and harbouring no sense of ownership of their school or what happens to or in it.

That this sad state of affairs persists not only reflects a critical waste of talent but also the possibility of serious social deviance. It also represents a colossal wastage of precious educational investment and non-use of human capital.

Because even as, inarguably, a midnight of the social and moral order sweeps the land (evidenced by an abundance of decay and decadence everywhere), schools should be a part of the solution, and not, as seems to obtain too often, a part of the problem.

Too many of our students are dropping out of schools - for a variety of reasons - before/without completing the full formal foundational- learning cycle. And clearly, many of them are gravitating towards a life of violence and sociopathy..

Leaders in education, parents and others in authority over children/students must know and act upon the fact that research after research, and study after study find that children as early as age three will have learnt and often exhibit the traits that can and do lead them into violence not many years later in their lives.

By age six, in fact, it is possible to predict fairly accurately which children will end up being aggressively violent, unless adequate, relevant intervention is forthcoming.

In schools, violence of whatever ilk corrupts the body politic. It is like a malignant microbe that eats away at the fabric of the school' essential constitution, and seriously limits the potential and efficacy of the teaching-learning exercise.

The omnipresent diet of violence galore on television, in the movies and the media contributes significantly to the orgy of violent conduct among our young people in general, and spilling over, naturally, in the school system.

These audios and visuals in no small way heighten opportunities for violence, as opposed to pro-social modelling. Of course, a child/student can only regurgitate what it is fed, and build with the tools at his disposal, thus, inevitably, violence rears its ugly head in our schools, which were once respected institutions of peaceful teaching and learning.

The cultural conditioning to which our students are subject consists of much reference, exposure and resort to violence.
This occurs in our homes, workplaces, where we go for pleasure and entertainment, in our films, movies, music, language, and public as well as private spaces.

No wonder it is so very present in our schools.

"Nothing lowers the level of conversation than raising the voice."

Creating Good Schools: - A Developmental Imperative

Schools in the Federation are currently on their annual summer vacation. It is a time when DESERVING students and teachers are allowed a break from the demands and dictates, stresses and challenges of the formal teaching- learning routine.

It is also an opportune time, no doubt, to assess the impact and success of schools as it relates to student attitude, behaviour, performance and achievement. These, in turn, indicate the level of teacher competence and effectiveness. Together, these determine whether a school is a good or poor school.

The question, then, is, in essence: Do the result of our students' performance on internal and external exams, their attitude and approach to education, and their behaviour and conduct, including care of the school premises and facilities, suggest that we have good schools? Is the philosophical platform of principals, which, in large measure, acts to shape their style of leadership and management, conducive to the creating and sustaining of good schools?

Are our schools able to present a record of success and effectiveness, which bodes well for national development? Do we have good schools? What makes for a good school?

A good school deports and comports certain characteristics that poor or mediocre schools clearly lack.

Good schools are determined by what is taught, how it is taught, and by whom. Such schools offer and impart to their clients - the students, the nation's most precious resource and valuable asset – relevant, meaningful and needed social, technical, technological and psycho-social skills. Their curricula involve a practical blend of sports, academic disciplines, arts, and opportunities for experiment and discovery.

Good schools, via the taught, caught, open and hidden curricula, afford their students the enabling environment to explore, develop and hone their talents, gifts and competencies, via an emphatic embrace of the multiple intelligences paradigm.

The students therein are guided, counselled and

husbanded into areas and disciplines that best conduce to their individual innate abilities, tastes, preferences and desires re careers.

Good schools exercise a robust discipline regime, with fair, sensible rules and regulations impartially, consistently and judiciously applied without fear or favour, malice or ill will. Safety and security of students, teachers, auxiliary workers, equipment, facilities and supplies are strictly honoured in the observance and practice.

The quality of the teacher staff occupies paramountcy in good schools. Here, teachers are knowledgeable, amenable to training, fair, just and compassionate, and readily contribute time, energy, ideas, support and other resources to the organization and execution of all school functions, events and operations. Teachers in good schools respect all students - and their parents -, and are dedicated to the proposition that all students can learn.

In good schools, the leadership is of excellent calibre, with a track record of involvement, reliability, and purpose. The administration and management of the institution is hallmarked by vision, passion, and action. The style of headship is neither crude nor infantile, displaying rather the principles of maturity and professional sophistication. Their level of autonomy allows them to be innovative, creative and flexible, engaging periodically in reflection and introspection. They set the tone and pace of/for the climate and culture of the school, inspiring their students and teachers to heights of superlative excellence, while nurturing strong bonds of co-operation, collaboration and partnership with all stakeholders and shareholders in the education enterprise, especially those more immediately connected to their particular school.

A system of monitoring of school inventories, school safety, school record, teacher performance, student conduct and performance, stakeholder support and general school progress is deliberately and conscientiously implemented as a matter of course.

Good schools adequately prepare students, who, of course, represent the rising generation, for the world of work, the marketplace, adulthood and parenting. The roles, rights and responsibilities of students as workers, parents and adults are emphasized, explained and modelled here.

Good schools output students with a worldview; ideal citizens driven by a spirit of ambition and industry, possessed of a keen sense of respect, responsibility and rectitude. In this connection, their emotional intelligence is addressed, cultural norms are exemplified, local history is promoted, and the need for / benefits of teamwork and collegiality are stressed: taught by precept and by example.

Good schools are necessary for sustainable development. Only good schools can seriously or significantly contribute to national cohesion, stability and progress.

Our collection investments in schools, expending as we do scarce resources of all types in and on them, legitimize our expectations, and our demands, that our schools be good schools.

Good schools attract attention and support. They befriend success, which generates its own momentum for more success. Right-thinking, concerned parents gravitate towards good schools.

It is important, critically, that good schools define ours. Where good schools do not exist because of poor leadership, for example a, new set of heads must replace those whose record is one of shame and failure. Where the reason is that of location, inadequate resources, poor teacher stock, or other factors, these must be addressed and corrected as a matter of urgency. Certainly in time for the beginning of the new school year in September.

As we analyze the product/output of schools over the past year(s), we must determine to do whatever it takes to ensure that henceforth, the very pertinent question, "Do we have good schools?", is ever answered, is only answerable, in the affirmative!

Let's Talk Schools - Again

Schools are just about starting out on a new academic year, 2016-2017.

Will it be business as usual? Can it be business as usual? Or will the course of the school year give birth to many - or any - of the new innovations and paradigms that so loudly and clearly beckon, and are sorely needed?

It seems apparent that superficially-presented statistics re pass rates, etc., notwithstanding, our education system as currently constituted faces a clear and present danger of falling short, perhaps far short of what is expected of modern education systems in democratic, developing mini-states such as ours in the 21st century.

Indeed, stalwart educator and social commentator and activist Washington Archibald (Washie), after and for whom our largest secondary school is named, in an article in the 'Observer Newspaper' in June, argued that murders - perhaps the most feared of all crimes, and the litmus test of a society's moral fibre, or lack of it - begin at school.

We may choose to mount that particular platform of contention, or not, but we cannot properly defenestrate the fact that, even with the watering down of passing grades at CXC exams (and we shall discuss that later) , an in-depth analysis of our students' performance reveals an abundance of poor quality passes and high numbers of outright failures. And even among those with the top-most grades, the general level of and calibre of speaking, writing, attitude and conduct do NOT at all reflect the standard and stature normally expected of students sporting such 'academic success'.

In fact, it is well known that many a Grade 'A' or '1' student so achieves as a result of 'extra lessons', 'shadow education', and cramming, just to 'pass the exam'. The need to memorize, then, and to regurgitate, has conspicuously replaced the impulse and the necessity to understand.

Of course, the fact that many students who begin secondary level education fail to complete it, coupled with the truth that many of our male students suffer from a systematic, biased bent that favours females in the education sector, continues to bedevil our efforts at creating and providing an inclusive education that benefits all equally, and to render shallow our boast of educational excellence.

Too many students leave the formal education process bereft of adequate thinking, reasoning, analytical, spatial, vocational, technical, literary and literacy skills.

These days, we hear talk of the living school concept, and of the child-friendly school. Essentially, these purport to create an environment wherein students are safe, secure, respected, assisted and supported in pedagogically-tested and sound ways that conduce to optimum learning and facilitate their holistic development.

Of course, these should be the normal characteristics that typify the climate, culture, practice and teaching modus operandi in our schools.

Perhaps this new school year will see a deliberate, determined, sustained effort to refocus the intentions, content, delivery, monitoring and evaluation of education, and insist on greater proficiency and accountability from practitioners and stakeholders in the education enterprise.

School, after all, is a teaching-learning institution. It is a socializing agent. It is a catalyst of change. It is an exemplar of moral purpose. It is an enabler of making a living. It is a trainer for the workplace. It is a 'ready-er' for adulthood. It is a place to build capacity to contribute to national development. It is a preparation for life.

Getting students to 'pass the exam' is but a miniscule aspect of the school's overall charge and function.

Let us together rally and demand that schools produce, that they be good schools. And of course, let us just as readily stir ourselves to contribute the ideas and the resources requisite for this demand to be realised.

We desperately need for the 2016-2017 school year to be the beginning of the end of the same old, same old, which, clearly, has been weighed in the balances and found wanting.

The Case for Moral Instruction in Schools.

Again and again, many persons of all strata, have loudly decried a rise in juvenile deviance (crime and delinquency), and as a (partial) corrective measure, announced a desire and an intention to introduce – re-introduce, some say - moral instruction in government schools.

This, it was hoped, would serve to stem the tide of violence amongst our youth, which ebbs and flows as parents and, apparently, teachers as well, seemingly lose the ability, or even the will, to control the behaviour of their children/wards.

Will moral instruction in schools stand the test of time? Are schools the proper locale for this intervention? Schools, of course, are but a microcosm of society. By and large, what happens in society is mirrored in the school. There, human feeling, activity and behaviour, circumscribed by routine and somewhat restrained by law, custom and etiquette, transpire with as much intensity as in any centre of business, and are the hallmarks of school life, just as they are of life in the adult world.

School is a melting pot of social attitudes and values, where real children of truly diverse backgrounds find a central meeting point. It is a hive of activity wherein a new generation is bred, instructed and formed. It is a hothouse of growth and development which, significant to this debate, encompasses the turbulent, some say, period of puberty and adolescence, wherein the flux of human nature becomes transformed into maturing personalities.

Perhaps this was a major consideration driving the decision of the 'movers and shakers'. If children become adults void of moral instruction, their future, our future, society's future, is bleak at best.

Formal education occurs at a time of life when students are passing through a period of rapid change. It is a time not to let slip by just like that.

And this begs the question: Is moral instruction potentially useful in shaping and influencing these changes in a socially-desired direction?

Many educators contend that schools have basically a four-fold mission: the academic-intellectual mission; the vocational-preparation mission; the inter-personal, co-operative mission (that is, the development of the student as a member of the community); and the personal moral development mission.

It would appear, from the raison d'être of the decision makers' concerns, that whereas whether the school may effectively be executing the first three named missions is debatable, that it has failed – woefully so - to deliver with respect to the last-named mission needs neither defence nor explanation.

Many would indeed agree that the content of our current education system essentially loads students with information and facts, but short-changes them in the critical areas of ethical and moral development.

The result? Young people lacking compassion, industry, and integrity; resistance to authority; violence-prone; and profoundly selfish. Morally bankrupt, in short.

So that (re) introducing moral instruction, in this scenario, must be construed as a step in the right direction.

Only if it works.

Educators and teachers in particular must grasp the gravity and profundity of this vision. The proponents of moral instruction are in fact declaring that the foci of education must change. No longer is education's major role merely to produce individuals who can participate in the economic structures of modern society. It must not even be confined to increasing the ability of individuals to appreciate and contribute to the cultural heritage of the land.

Its function must now of necessity expand to include facilitating the unfolding of the spiritual potential, the manifestation of which includes a sense of moral rectitude, which lies innate within the breast of every adult and child on the Earth.

If this potential is harnessed as is ought I, dare foresay that much of the sociopathic behaviours that presently bedevil our schools and contaminate our society, would cease.

Teachers, therefore, must now be able to communicate not just brain food, but soul food; not just mind to mind, but heart to heart.

Henceforth, a conscientious and deliberate effort must be made to replace, or at least de-emphasise and dilute the self oriented and material values and tastes which saturate and dominate the lives of most of the student body today.

Moral instruction must take the students in a direction that leads to a philosophy of tolerance and inclusion; to a life of deeper meaning and purpose. The current almost-mechanical process of a blind perpetuation of crystallised, egoistic values must give way to a new dispensation of a creative dynamic exercise that combines all four missions in an efficient, effective manner that redounds to the mutual benefit of all the stakeholders and shareholders in the education enterprise.

Of course, I do not, I cannot claim that the development of the intellect is inadequate in itself. But the present large focus on training the memory almost solely for the purpose of 'getting a good job' is itself so inadequate that even the blind can see, especially when juxtaposed against the larger perspective of a more comprehensive understanding of the constitution, potential and totality of the human being.

After all, the said human being is essentially a spiritual being. Yet this dimension of his persona is generally seriously neglected in the pursuit of satisfying of the social aspect of his humanity.

The student is not just a receptive void waiting to be filled with 'education'; he is a living, thinking individual seeking assistance and guidance to develop his entire personhood. The role of the teacher, then, is to introduce the atmosphere and impart the content, in word and in deed, whereby this development may be best facilitated.

So, many concerned persons insist we need moral instruction to help redress the imbalance which now so heavily favours the negative trends and behaviours among our youths, the rising generation.

I say, let's have it! May it succeed where its absence has failed so miserably.

"Luck so often seems to be against those who depend on it."

"Life comprises getting and giving, forgetting and forgiving."

"If you consider your neighbor unpleasant, chances are he does, too."

EDUCATION

Everyone knows, of this I am sure, that Education is the key
That opens doors to insight, self-esteem, growth and prosperity.
It co-operates with intelligence to render a person mentally fit.
Education is such a potent asset; we should truly ever value it.

Education takes one smoothly, form nothingness to prominence,
Enabling him to move with ease from penury to affluence.
It turns bigots into brothers, makes an expert of an ignoramus.
Education facilitates improvement in all areas of human effort.

No other means or process, no other institution
Can effect the positive changes; can build, like Education.
Education should make better the way we think, move and conduct;
Education, therefore, more than any, ensures and presents a solid product.
In some countries, unfortunately, full access to Education
Is rather scarce and limited: This sure causes retrogression.
For even if, as some contend, Education is expensive,
Its opposite, which is ignorance, is far, far more ineffective!

Here in St. Kitts and Nevis, true, we've had Universal Education,
At Primary and Secondary levels, with tertiary heading for fruition.
We therefore ought to appreciate, exploit, apply and cherish,
Our free access to Education; without it, we're bound to perish.

Teaching and Education in this Age: Trials and Challenges

It is manifestly the case at this critical juncture of our socio-politico-historical development that education including – its process, objectives, modus operandi and outcomes --, its outstanding instances of unparalleled success notwithstanding, is proving to be woefully ineffective in many other glaring instances.

Of course, specific educational problems vary according to a people's needs and culture, yet local states of affairs must be seen and addressed in the context of the global environs, given the universality of education that is so profoundly becoming more pronounced.

Certainly, one can point without fear of contradiction to a number of ills and wrongs in the education arena. For one, the ageless adage that we teach loudest and best by example rather than by precept seems lost on very many of our teachers. After all, good teaching is not at all only a matter of specific or even effective techniques, styles of plans of actions. It is very essentially a matter of vision, discipline and love.

In our schools today, significant numbers of our teachers and students alike fail in their duties and endeavours because of a deep material as well as spiritual poverty; and the capacity to be educated, edified and illumined, found innate in every human being, is stifled because of the perpetuating tendency to enclose learners within the framework of an ideal that that simply encourages, often coerces them to conform, rather than discover and create.

Admittedly, the failing of the school system cannot be seen, examined or understood in a vacuum. After all, all of society's major institutions are failing, some falling, at times miserably and rapidly,

Some argue that the education which provided order, security, stability, and the wherewithal for individual and national progress is no longer adequate to our 'new' awareness, maturity and sophistication.

One wonders whether education's and schools' traditional emphasis on order, discipline, obedience to authority, diligence, industry, and respect for the opinions, person and property of others, number among the 'old' set of values that has no place in the ultra-modern 21st century.

For what we are seeing now, more than ever, as typical of our 'young' people, is plenteousness of disrespect, aggression and violence, and an abundance of lack of tolerance, challenge to authority, insolence, and quick resort to blaming others.

All this anarchic behaviour against the background of heavy emphasis and expenditure on matters educational by the central government, super-emphasis on doing things for and aimed at 'youth', providing almost all the material that should facilitate success in education free of cost, a plethora of laws that support and promote youth, and a growing trend to include 'young' people in decision-making and responsible positions.

One is therefore left to wonder whether the full development of the human personality that education seeks to effect, includes, among other manifestations, wearing grossly-oversized pants on the bottom instead of on the waist (in the case of males), and, in the case of females, sporting skirts that are shorter than time and as tight as a knot.

Yes, education brings freedom, or so it ought. But certainly not freedom to be violent, criminal, intolerant and inconsiderate.

Again, one questions the link between behaviours, attitudes and performance of contemporary 'youth' – students in particular - , and severe teacher shortages in several countries, while in so many others, myriad persons use teaching as a sort of bridge to other 'higher', less stressful, more rewarding jobs and professions.

Emerging educational models consider human as opposed to curriculum development; measures progress by HOW WELL and not WHAT students learn ; espouses teaching not via lectures and textbooks, but by exploring multisensory information; and focuses on empowering rather than controlling the learner.

Yet these new paradigms at the same time seem to cultivate a culture that glorifies materialism, competition, and self-aggrandizement, while annihilating respect for innocence, purity and rectitude of a moral order.

The challenge before us as teachers in the 21st century is to ensure that education for this new era is fully holistic, and builds capacity for understanding the inter-connectedness of life on the planet. Certainly, no child is born a drop-out, genius, terrorist, statesman, PAM, Labour, PLP, Fascist or Democrat. Children, students and people become what circumstances, socialization and the environment make them. Children construct with what they are given and with what they can find.

If the material is poor, or the tools inadequate, so will be the construction.

As teachers, our task is clear.

"Don't die until you are dead."

"No matter how dirty and stained is a man's past, the future is spotless."

Quality Teachers for Quality Education - The Global Imperative

It is manifestly the case today that quality - in whatever field of endeavour - is far more often than not, an objective, a state of being more ardently to be desired than seriously to be expected. For far too long, we have acquiesced to a decline in standards of all sorts, and have embraced mediocrity, or worse, as acceptable, even sufficient. Indeed, on a regular basis, we tend to christen as 'excellent' that which is far from so.

And this sorry state of affairs afflicts the process of education and affects the noble profession of teaching at least as much as it does other fields of human activity.

Education is, of course, a life-long exercise in learning, resulting, as it ought, in individuals changing their behaviour, attitudes and outlook as they are impacted by this process.

The importance, in fact the utter indispensability of Education as a medium of and basis for growth, development and progress at the personal and international level in these ultra-modern times has long being settled, is unquestioned.

Education promotes strategic mobility for capacity building. It develops a person's ability to make decisions that will affect and improve himself. It is the pivot on which society's unending thrust forward rotates.

And yet there can be little real education, let alone quality education, without teachers. Teachers are, beyond dispute, the most vital component of the formal education system.

It is certainly not difficult to visualize the utter chaos that society would degenerate into if there were no doctors, ministers of government and religion, engineers, teachers, bankers, businessmen, security personnel, accountants, pilots, etc.

Well, who do you think gave all these very important people their knowledge, information and skills? Who do you think taught and prepared them? The answer might shock some of you! Teachers – good, quality teachers!

So that teachers, and the education whose assimilation and accommodation they facilitate, are intimately related to issues beyond the boundaries of the classroom, country or region. Small wonder, then, that the CARICOM Single Market and Economy, for example, arranges for the free movement of professional teachers in the Community, as one of its central tenets.

The truth, however, is that there is strong legitimate concern whether the educational content and process of our small nation-states embraces and is characterized by relevance and meaningfulness.

I submit, in fact, that it is education and teachers which must be the main tool for achieving and effectively managing the pluralism in society, the demands of the technological age we inhabit, and the economic changes which globalization implies. With education, barriers to upward mobility and marketability fall, the playing field is levelled, and one becomes equipped to make a more robust contribution to his community and civilization, whilst propelling himself forward, upward and onward.

Quality education, therefore, must create not just an awareness, but a proper understanding of the workings of global phenomena, which, from all appearances, are here to stay, even as they constantly evolve and mutate.

However, education thus far has generally involved much blind perpetuation of old and crystallized values. It has largely focused on training the memory and developing the intellect largely for the purpose of "passing the exam" and "getting a good job". But certainly, this cannot suffice.

Quality education, then, does not solely seek to produce individuals bent on perpetuating the socio-cultural-economic norms of the day. It enables persons rather to anticipate, manipulate and participate in the changing social, cultural, political and economic structures of the modern global village. It engages the whole person right from the start, enhancing his ability to appreciate and contribute to the cultural heritage of humanity, and to unfold his innate, latent spiritual potential.

Quality education essays to dispense with mediocrity, especially when excellence is within grasp. It produces an infinite capacity to bear the pain necessarily involved in the striving for excellence. Surely, it takes hard work to achieve quality education, and more hard work to keep it going, but then, quality teachers, and they only, are the ones to facilitate its realization. Quality teachers produce quality teaching. They are committed to honesty, morals, values, respect, tolerance, peace and non-violence, order, discipline, decency, compassion, industry, justice, healthy living, national pride, selfishness, and success, among other critical values.

These experts lend a lie to George Bernard Shaw's aphorism that "He who can, does; He who cannot, teaches." Quality teachers not only can, they do it with class! To be a quality teacher requires and involves a special talent, and a sense of vocation. Such a one tells, explains, demonstrates and inspires. His personal prejudices, idiosyncrasies and welfare are subsumed by his consideration for and interest in his wards' needs and circumstances.

In the constructing of the edifice of the students' talents, skills, attitudes, knowledge and information, the quality teacher recognizes and acknowledges that he is not the builder per se, but more so the collaborator in the building process. He permits the learner to see what globalization and world developments are and mean, how education operates, how to make it work to his benefit and that of his community, how to become a key player rather than just be an affected spectator. This, so that the unsatisfactory (high) levels of insularity, crime and violence, polarization, persistent poverty, incivility, sociopathic behaviour, lop-sided economies, mal-governance and other ills that characterize his existence and surroundings, can be reduced, in the very least.

Clearly, then, quality teachers and quality education are closely related. Inextricably interwoven, even. Together, they enrich the teaching-learning enterprise, and strengthen the education system.

It therefore behoves all the stakeholders and shareholders in this endeavour, including, in particular, Government, the Teachers' Union and individual teachers, to recognize and act upon the foregoing. Adversarial relationships between employer and employee, between 'management and labour', and amongst employees themselves can only exert a negative drag on quality and productivity, and eventually, adulterate the body politic.

An atmosphere of trust, respect, partnership and excellence, however, attracts quality teachers and augments quality education.

Are our teachers quality teachers? Are they involved in quality teaching? If the truth to be told, more than just a few fail the test. Yet, they have a moral interpretive and professional duty to be both.

After all, the fate of society, present and future, depends on what and how well its younger citizens are taught today. The hope of the human race lies chiefly in quality education. Lets us be a part of it.

"Efficiency: accomplishing more with less exertion and fewer expenses."

"Flirtation is attention without intention."

Peer Mediation & Resolution - A Paradigm Shift in Managing Conflict in Schools

Our schools are a microcosm of society, an eclectic mix of temperaments, attitudes and beliefs shaped by familial upbringing and socialisation, and influenced by environment and experience.

Schools are hive of activity, wherein the flux of human nature manifests itself uninterruptedly and without regard, in multiple ways and forms.

The diverse socio-economic, cultural, religious and, less pronouncedly, ethnic background of the students, dictates necessarily, that these diversities colour and characterise school life, especially as it pertains to behaviour.

At times, inevitably, almost inexorably, theses difference in style and substance lend and lead to misunderstandings, miscalculations, intolerance, impatience, conflict and strife.
In fact, the quintessential feature of school life is conflict among and between students, and the never-ending effort of teachers to contain it.

It is indeed absolutely critical that those persons, who act in loco parentis for as long as the students are in their care and charge, address these conflicts frontally, as failure to do so facilitates a rapid descent into bacchanal, confusion, chaos and crime, which, together and separately, render the teaching-learning process unsafe, insecure, self-defeating and counter-productive. By extension / amplification, the huge investments made in the education sector by the Government become a wasted exercise / expense.

In recent times, the nature, scope, equality and frequency of instances of conflict and strife have witnessed a change, one that sees such instances reflecting a clear flavour of deviance, at times bordering on, and indeed, involving criminality, pure and simple.

This problem is made no less intractable by the convergence of a number of factors, including: The gross and stultifying delinquency / irresponsibility of many far too many parents in effectively training, disciplining, guiding and controlling their children

The growing pervasive negative influences and uses of the (especially) electronic media, including the internet, cell and i-phones, and television.

An increasing and troubling tendency on the part of many students to openly defy, flout, challenge and threaten the authority of parents, teachers, the police, and society in general, with no concern for or fear of penalty

Numerous instances of the juvenile and criminal justice system seeming to be extra and ultra-lenient ,almost to the point of being dismissive or tolerant in their treatment of so-called juvenile offenders.

A growing frustration on the part of many teachers - including principals - in dealing with conflict among students, which is due to several factors. These include;

Growing levels of aggression and violence flowing from students.

Much recidivism

Improper and inadequate security

A perception that the Ministry of Education is either unable or unwilling, or both, to lend the necessary moral, legislative, legal, personnel and material support to stem the tide.

A drive to lessen and restrict dramatically the use of the 'rod' or strap as an instrument of correction

The subtle and not-so-subtle influence of the gang culture on students.

A general conspicuous decline in the moral and civil quality of society at large.

Of course, time and repeatedly, again and again, in forum after forum, much discussion transpires involving the various stakeholders in education, which includes very much all sectors of the body politic, including schools, parents, the business and religious community, law enforcement, civil society, community volunteer organizations, and government as well as non-governmental organizations, inter alia.

Yet, while much rhetoric abounds, conflict and strife in our schools continually ebb and flow.

Over the years, much reliance has been placed on the application of corporal punishment, suspension and expulsion as major means of responding to incidents flowing from strife and conflict in the schools.

Clearly, while these traditional methods may have effectively served their purpose in times past, it is patently transparent that new strategies must be designed and adopted today.

In the circumstances, therefore, the MOE should opt for Peer Mediation as one such new approach.

Peer Mediation (PM) seeks to recognize and arrange the emotional turmoil that many researchers seem to agree define the period of growth that occurs during compulsory school age (5 - 16 years).

The mediator does not play the role of police officer, judge or counsellor, but facilitates communication so that the disputants themselves can find a solution.

PM admits that educating the heart is as important as educating the mind, otherwise geniuses will use their knowledge unwisely, for evil, even; and morons will be moral degenerates.

PM allows students themselves to be directly and actively engaged in the process of solving conflict problems of behaviour and actions.

It affords them the privilege to decide the outcome of conflicts and disputes involving their peers.

It reduces to a minimum the hitherto predominantly-teacher-directed decision-making, which often smacks of being partial, whimsical, arbitrary and/or unilateral, and is shaped by a vertical rather than a horizontal approach.

Instead, it offers a whole-school approach, honing and exploiting the intrinsic strengths and capacity of students in matters of negotiation, civility, decency, impartiality, anger management, conflict resolution and self-control.

Towards this end, PM engages students in much role-playing as a means of confirming their skills of non-judgmental questioning, active listening, and conscious presence.

PM develops in students the art of openness, a critical ingredient for justice to be fair and just.

PM advocates not just punitive or retributive justice, but restorative justice as well.

For PM, as a novel and innovative introduction on the school scene, to be effective, impactful and enviable, it must be propelled by the momentum of its own success, and find resonance in the minds and hearts of the student populace at large.

Students, more specifically student leaders, must be trained, which involves ample case studies being presented.

Reference material, stationery supplies and a designated 'PM centre' must be made available. These include mediation and negotiation workbooks, DVD's, and, where recommended, pedagogic instruments.

There must also be a commitment on the part of the school administration and staff to support the PM regime.

It is believed that PM adds value to the education enterprise, and creativity to the teaching learning exercise, as it transports the theory of student participation to the domain of action and reality.

It is also believed that if PM in St. Kitts is introduced on a seriatim basis, and is first piloted for a year in a primary and a secondary school (simultaneously); if it is subsequently robustly evaluated, it could in fact be an appropriate response mechanism to the ongoing challenge of confronting the twin evils of strife and conflict in schools.

There is a widespread general tendency for students to be, at the very least, tacitly supportive of their peers, even when they (admit they) are wrong. The typical 'rule' is that students remain silent when asked by a teacher/principal to identify one of their peers as a culprit.

It is therefore hoped that youths, students, will be more amenable and apt to accept the judgment of their peers, whom, they believe - rightly or wrongly - are more in sync with and understanding of the unique experiences, sentiments, emotions, desires and expectations characteristic of their stage/phase of development.

May peer mediation succeed where its predecessors have failed, and/or are failing, miserably. The Objectives of the Peer Mediation and Anger Management Programme will be:

To assist students in:

Understanding how anger is seen in our culture
Understanding that anger can be positive or negative
Understanding the origins of anger - hurt, denial, put down, shut down, let down by others, including their very peers
Understanding themselves and their feelings
Understanding some of the psychological/social issues around anger
Accepting that personality/parenting/behavioural issues can contribute to one's feelings of anger
Building awareness of why students do what they do
Learning how to seek and accept help in managing anger.

To assist teachers and Guidance Counsellors in:

Understanding how Emotional Literacy can inhibit violent behaviour

Building more positive relationships among students

Acknowledging and recognising how "acting-out" behaviour can spiral out of control

Understanding the roots of anger and conflict

Working with students and their families in managing anger

Understanding how they can contribute to negative anger.

To assist parents and guardians in:

Providing support to teachers and their children

Understanding anger and conflict issues

Developing the ability to look for signs of potential trouble in children.

Beneficiaries

Students
Teachers
Guidance Counsellors
Schools
Parents/Guardians
General Public

Expected Impact

Students will become better able to: understand their emotions, manage their emotions and anger, manage potential conflict situations, look for alternatives to violent behaviour, build peace-giving and peace-sharing initiatives, and choose discussion and sharing of feelings, instead of violence.

Teachers, Guidance Counsellors and parents/guardians will become better able to: understand how emotional issues impact children and adults, understand how to listen and how to detect potential trouble, assist children in sharing their feelings, provide support to students in finding alternatives to violence, minimize potential conflict situations , and seek help without feeling weak or humiliated. Ultimately, these initiatives should lead, in the short to medium term, to a reduction in the incidence of school violence in secondary schools, and in the long term to a reduction of violence in society.

Main Activities

The Peer Mediation and Anger Management Programme will consist of the following components:
A training programme for teachers and students in secondary schools and two last grades of primary schools
The provision of a teacher's guide for teaching or handbook
Training programme for parents/guardians
Distribution of handbook - "Managing Anger - Resolving Conflict via Peer Mediation" to teachers and students in the secondary schools and the two last grades of the primary schools.

A consultant will be identified to provide the following:

Presentation to students in all schools (promotion of the handbook)
Training workshops for teachers and students
Training workshops for parents/guardians (after school hours)

Follow-up focus group evaluation sessions with students in each school.

The teachers, guidance counsellors and parents/guardians workshops will include the following:

Understanding anger (negatives and positives of anger, anger and violence, impulse control, self esteem and anger)
Conflicts management (how conflict begins, how conflict spirals, how conflict can be managed)
Emotional literacy (the importance of emotional literacy, understanding why smart persons do dumb things, emotions, anger and feelings, how students can be taught how to avoid violence, providing alternatives for students, and involving parents/guardians in the discussion).

Lesson planning on 'Managing Anger' and 'Conflict Resolution'..

Following completion of the training activities, there will be systematic monitoring and evaluation of student activities at regular intervals in about six months to a year to document and determine whether there is any significant reduction in the incidence of violence among children in the project schools.

Expected Results

The handbook, Managing Anger- Resolving Conflict, that will be used during the training will become a resource text for the curriculum for secondary schools and will be used by students, teachers and guidance counsellors
Anger Management/ Conflict Resolution will be a long-term subject for students in secondary schools.
Parents and guardians will be provided with information on how they could support the schools, so that what is taught at school could be re-enforced at home.

Students moving into secondary school will be sensitized at an early stage to the issues of Anger Management, Impulse Control and Conflict Resolution.

Teachers and Guidance Counsellors will be empowered and assisted in paying greater attention to Emotional Literacy, which will greatly enhance an understanding of violence, anger and "acting out" behaviour.

"Children embarrass us in public by behaving just as they do at home."

"If you are not mature enough to take criticism, you're too immature for praise."

"Be yourself, and you'll be at home anywhere."

Published by:

www.purposefulauthors.com

Affiliated with:

Author's Contact:

TEL: 1-869-669-0984

Email: sylvesterblake137@yahoo.com

www.ingramcontent.com/pod-product-compliance
Lightning Source LLC
Chambersburg PA
CBHW051827020726
47502CB00005B/1669